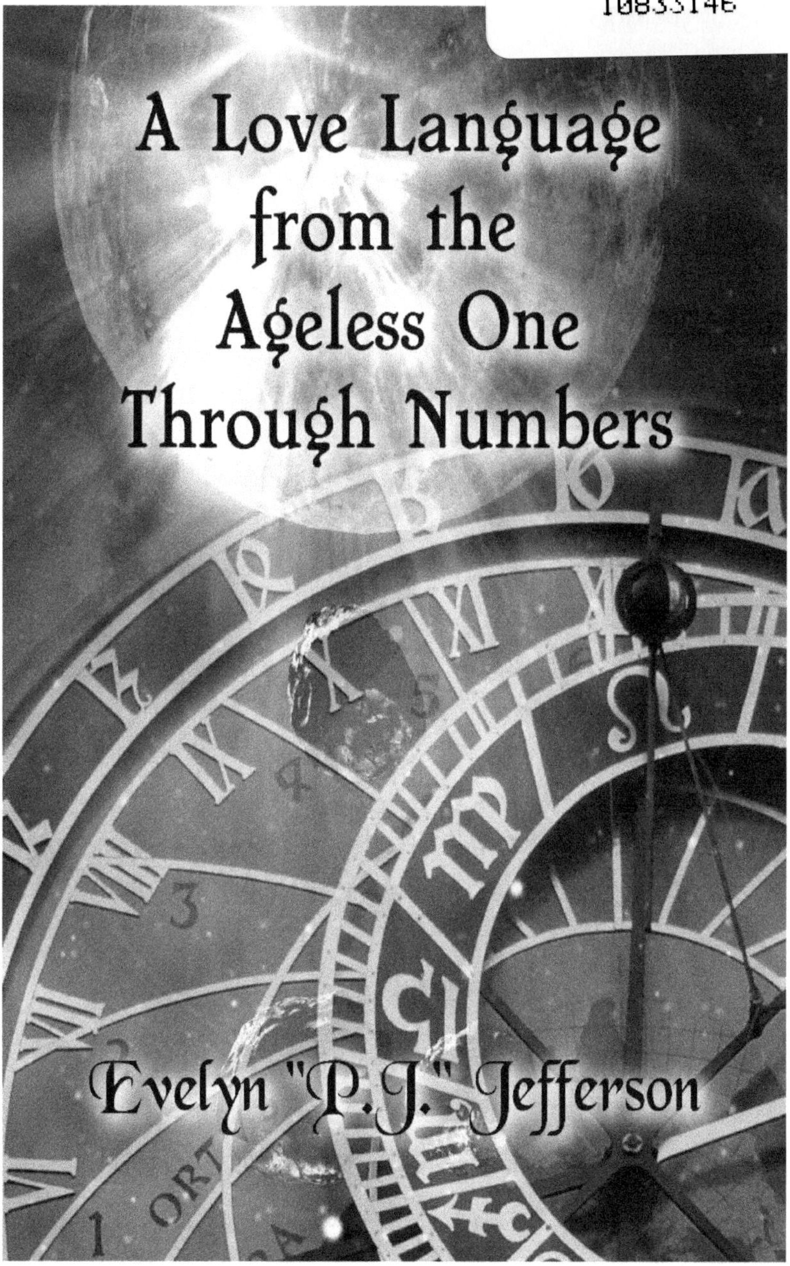

A Love Language from the Ageless One Through Numbers

Evelyn "P.J." Jefferson

Copyright/Title Page

A Love Language from the Ageless One Through Numbers

Published by: Books by L Mason: "A Safe Place"
P. O. Box 1162
Powhatan, VA 23139

Author: Evelyn "P. J." Jefferson
Cover Design: SelfPubBookCovers.com/RLSather

PJBlaze408@gmail.com

ISBN- 978-1-967205-50-9 (Color Paperback)
ISBN- 978-1-967205-51-6 (Blk & Wt Paperback)
ISBN- 978-1-967205-52-3 (Color Hardback)
LCCN: 2022912124

Printed in the United States of America

A Love

Language from the

Ageless One

Through

Numbers

Reveal Behind the Cover

This page is written to give you a mental picture of what I see, making this cover a "must-have" for this book. I firmly believe that those with an artistic eye, heart, and mind may see other things beyond what's here, but whether you see more, I didn't want anyone to see less than what a reveal "behind the cover" could provide.

Happy

Viewing,

From "P. J."

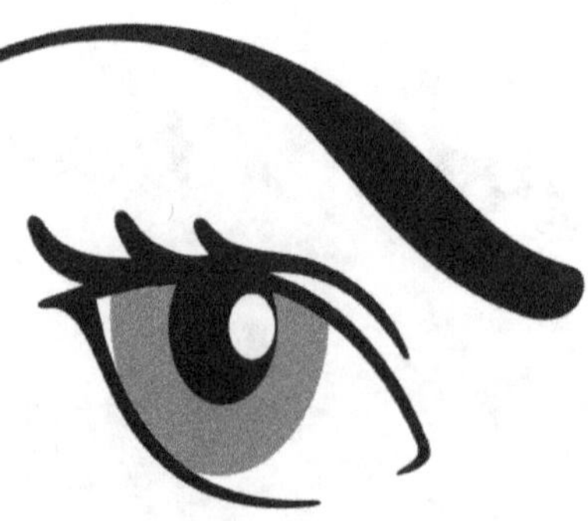

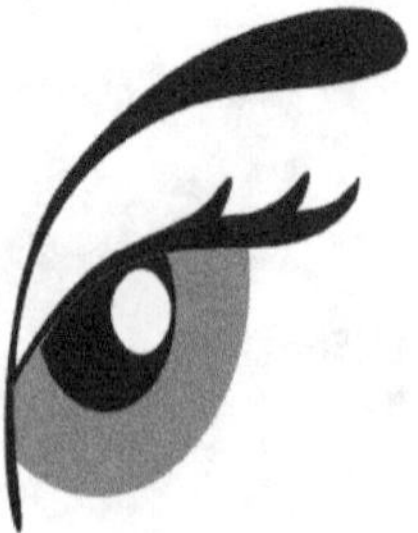

What immediately drew me to this cover were three elements.

- First, the appearance of brilliant light shining through to light up numbers on what seems to be an ancient timepiece
- Second, the ancient timepiece, possessing all manner of numbers: Roman numbers, foreign numbers, and everyday widely used numbers
- Third, the light piercing through what looks like a film of darkness shining on the timepiece numbers representing the ages

The timepiece's look held all elements of the title, "A Love Language from the Ageless One Through Numbers." In this book, you will discover that light represents revelation. The light shining through the timepiece on the cover speaks of the Ageless One, sending eye-opening revelations through time for us to embrace today.

Table of Contents

Copyright Page	ii
Reveal Behind the Cover	iv
Table of Contents	vi
Dedication	xi
Acknowledgments	xii
Foreword	xiv
The Birth of a Love Language	xvi
Birth of the Love Language Poem	xix
Explanatory Notes	xxi
❖ Acronyms vs. Acrostic Style Poetry	xxv
❖ Acrostic Style Poetry	xxvi
❖ The Possible Peace-filled Process	xxvii
❖ Are You Open to Fresh Reveals?	xxix
❖ Scriptures of Hidden Mysteries	xxix
❖ Because He Cares …	xxxii
❖ God---The Original Author	xxxiii
❖ Dear Reader	xxxv
The Ageless One Defined	xxxvi
Absolutely, "All Things Work"	xxxvii
Habakkuk 2:1	xxxviii
I Will Stand on My Watch	xxxix
Listen	xl

Table of Contents

Introduction	1
0/Zero	5
1/One	10
2/Two	15
3/Three	28
4/Four	38
5/Five	53
6/Six	70
7/Seven	75
8/Eight	85
9/Nine	92
10/Ten	105
11/Eleven	117
12/Twelve	128
13/Thirteen	137
14/Fourteen	143
15/Fifteen	153
16/Sixteen	163
17/Seventeen	167
18/Eighteen	173
19/Nineteen	184
20/Twenty	197
21/Twenty-One	208
22/Twenty-Two	211
23/Twenty-Three	220
24/Twenty-Four	222
25/Twenty-Five	235

Table of Contents

26/Twenty-Six 237
27/Twenty-Seven 240
28/Twenty-Eight 243
29/Twenty-Nine 245
30/Thirty 248
40/Forty 252
50/Fifty 254
10 Pictures of Who the He Is 255
The Number for The Holy Spirit 266
Jubilee 267
The Holy Spirit 269

- Comforter/Counselor 272
- Helper/Advocate 273
- Intercessor 274
- Strengthener/Standby 276
- Convicts/Convinces 277
- Condemner vs Convictor 278

The Holy Spirit is Your Good Conscience 279
Why Should You Care About Holy Spirit? 280
What Sets H. S. Apart from Other Spirits? 283
Why It's Important to Know Holy Spirit 285
He Understands Your Spiritual Need to Know 287
Number for Holy Spirit 289
Let It Rip!!! 293
The Solar Eclipse Identity Chart 296

Table of Contents

What and How You Think and Believe 299
The Three "Need to Know" Balances 301
Time 307
God's Reminder from the Clock 308
All Things in Life 315
How He Still Sees You 318
Negative to Positive 328
How Much He Cares and How Often 341
The Loving Message that Kisses Me to Sleep 343
Holy Spirit Is--- Just Ask. He's Waiting 345
Proof of the Sovereignty of God 349
ISBN Personified 351
The Difference Between a Testimony vs. A Glory Story 352
Testimonials of How He Speaks 355

1. Mental, Emotional 356
2. Mental, Emotional 359
3. Physical, Mental, Emotional 360
4. Spiritual, Relational 363
5. Spiritual, Physical, Mental, Emotional 364
6. Spiritual, Relational 366
7. Spiritual, Physical, Mental, Emotional 367
8. Spiritual, Natural, Mental, Emotional, 368
9. Spiritual, Recreational 372
10. Spiritual, Relational 375
11. Spiritual, Relational 376
12. Spiritual, Recreational 376
13. Physical, Mental, Emotional, Financial 378

Table of Contents

14. Spiritual, Relational 384
15. Physical, Mental, Emotional, Financial 388
16. Spiritual, Emotional 389
17. Mental, Emotional 389
18. Mental, Emotional, Financial 391
19. Spiritual, Mental, Emotional, Relational 395
20. Spiritual, Physical, Mental, Emotional 397
21. Spiritual 398
22. Spiritual, Mental, Emotional 401
23. Mental, Emotional, Opportunal 402
24. Spiritual, Mental, Emotional, Relational 403
25. Spiritual, Mental, Emotional, Relational 404
26. Spiritual, Opportunal 405
27. Spiritual, Relational, Recreational, Opp 407
28. Spiritual, Relational, Recreational, Opp 409
29. Spiritual, Relational 410
30. Spiritual, Relational, Recreational 411

For Those Who Need to Know 412
Matching Friend Request 419
Altar Call 421
I Will Stand On My Watch 422
Let's Prove to the Whole World 423
Afterword 424
Book Review 426
About the Author 428

Dedication

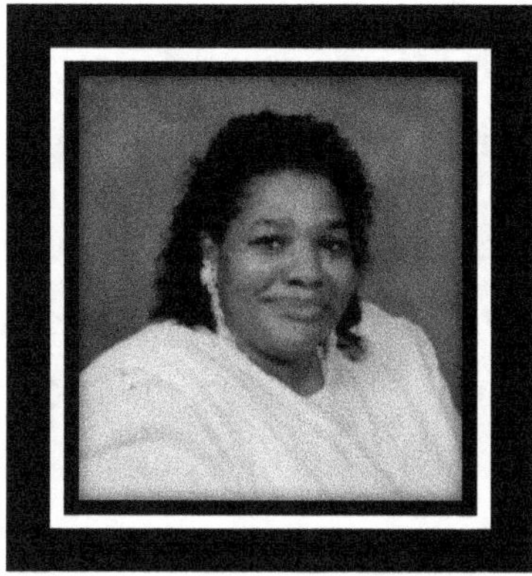

I dedicate this book "A Love Language from the Ageless One Through Numbers," to my mother, Dollie M. Jefferson, "The Late Great"

Unsung

Mathematician

in our family. She was magnificently gifted with numbers, and I know she is "tickled pink" to see how God has used numbers in such an intimate way, where numbers equal words of loving encouragement. Mom, you always said God had something special for me to reveal, and now your words have come to pass.

I Will Forever Love You

Acknowledgments

I want to start by lovingly acknowledging the One who made *everything* possible.

The Almighty Creator God
Our Everlasting Heavenly Father
My Papa Daddy God
"The Ageless One"

who gave me what I am sharing regarding *The Love Language Through Numbers*. I can't stop being in "awe" that You chose me to bring forth this "Gift of Love" from Your heart to Your created mankind. I could talk about You forever. I'm grateful that I know You know how much I love You.

I also want to acknowledge the gifts You gave me to help bring this love offering to life. Kalisha, my daughter, and Joshua, my grandson, who, like the rest of my family, has for years shared me with God and my writing pen as the time spent listening and writing was a sacrifice they lovingly made, knowing what God wanted to be done with my life. They recognized the importance of getting this book written so that others would have a chance to experience what they had seen God do in their own lives.

To my siblings, James "Redd," Bob, and Angie, with whom I live, I have appreciated your love, encouragement, jokes, and anticipation for this book to come to pass. To my big sister, Carol, who faithfully intercedes for all of us, and for me in particular, for my health and my ability to finish this book — thank you. This has meant so much to me.

Over the years, there have been those who would ask me what the numbers they encountered meant, but there were those who literally tugged on this book coming forth like a midwife during childbirth: Pattie Hertz, Karlene O'Connor, and Leona Gill, thank you. Pattie, the "Baby" is here!!!

Last but definitely not least is my sister Linda, who has encouraged, pushed, and used her gifts to help me bring this book and others into existence.

She is a one-woman
pep squad
that is the "*Duracell energizer bunny*"
when it comes to doing
whatever it takes
to get the things of God into a finished product.

I thank all who have been mentioned and all who were not.

A thank you to you, too!!!
I Love You,
My Darlings.

Foreword

My Introduction to "P.J." as an Insightful Author

Get ready to be blessed beyond measure with P.J.'s publication, "A Love Language from the Ageless One Through Numbers!" She genuinely enjoys encouraging everyone to know God personally and has proven it over the years through her spiritual writings and encouraging conversations. Over the decades, her relationship with God has always been paramount in our conversations concerning different topics. P.J.'s organic teachings from the Holy Spirit on how to deepen your intimacy with God by hearing Him speak to you through numbers will deepen your trust in God, knowing He loves and cares about everything you do. Her personal relationship with God will make you jealous of wanting to be closer to Him as you read this book.

For decades, I have had the pleasure of reading and being blessed by P.J. Jefferson's inspirational writings. I always knew that P.J. was a writer, and our conversations included mention of her journals. After my husband died in 2018, I saw a glimpse of the depth of P.J.'s spiritual insight in her writing. She wrote an exemplary inspirational poem about my husband's personality and how she saw him through the eyes of our heavenly Father. She also prepared one for each of our children and grandchildren. I could not have articulated it any better. She knew him through years of working with us in ministry and provided continued support with calls, prayers, and a hospital visit during his years of physical struggles. A few years later, she wrote a beautiful poem celebrating my mother's 90th birthday. I am forever grateful, especially for her unconditional love and support for my family.

Written by Pattie Hertz/ 2022
Motivational Speaker and Author
of "Daily Living"

The Birth of a Love Language

You may have wondered how this form of communication came to be and how it became such a vital part of my daily life —so essential — that I totally trust sharing this numbers love language with all of you. I'll start by telling you I had a "death-to-life" experience approximately twelve years ago.

My daughter told me that during a family gathering, I was sitting in a chair talking when I let out a cry, turned gray, and died on the spot. She told me that after they had gotten me to the floor and as she was praying, she started to attempt to revive me; she heard and felt the breath of God pass her face and enter into my nostrils. She said, "Mom, other people who are revived inhale to catch their breath, but you exhaled the breath of God."

During my recovery, the faith-filled, encouraging promises I would hear from God would now be attached to numbers I encountered. He would illuminate them in the eyes of my heart. What started as one or two-word messages turned into whole conversations. For example,

<u>19, which can mean peace</u>
when spotlighted, became an instruction I could hold on to.
I would hear, "Stay calm."

At another time, the numbers
<u>1914, which in this case</u>
I heard, "Stay calm. I'm healing you, and all is well."

As I embraced the messages, their power would be released to help me get through whatever I was facing.

During the years that followed, there have been countless horrific incidents that I've lived through. There have been many death-threatening struggles at home, multiple hospital stays, and multiple trips to the emergency room, to name a few. But, the constant peace-invoking things He gave me to take my mind off the threats and fears were to "look at the numbers and listen to His voice."

I was taught how to hear from God through the love language of multiple combinations of numbers He shared with me. Everything held a number message that could relieve me from anxiety overtaking me and causing me to exasperate the situation with being too stressed out to participate in anything that would help me; the number of the ambulance that transported me, how many EMTs came to help, and blood pressures that were taken on the way to the hospital even though some were exaggeratedly through the roof and threatened to stroke me out.

Papa God would let me see and hear in His number language that all those numbers did not represent destruction for me. This included the cubicle they assigned me in the E.R., the unit, floor, and the room I ended up in. And even the numbers for measuring fluid intake/output were all highlighted to me. Every number or set of numbers spoke of what God wanted me to concentrate on until His promises manifested enough for me to go home.

I could share hundreds, if not thousands, of examples with you, revealing how I became sure of His communications with me, but that would require a never-ending book. Just know that there's no doubt when I hear from God through numbers that He is speaking direction, love, and life to my heart, body (literally), and soul. He speaks often, and He speaks truth. So, I do not doubt that He could speak often and speak the truth to you, too.

Birth of the Love Language

Brought forth
Into
Reality from
The
Heart of God to

Offer
Forever Love and Friendship

To
Hungry hearts that are
Eager to know that there is someone who

Longs to
Open their eyes to have faith to
Venture into an
Encounter with Him who

Loves them most
And
Never again fear that
God doesn't
Understand
All about what
Gives them pause of
Entering into a relationship with Him

A scripture in the Bible says, "He (God) would keep you in perfect peace whose mind is stayed on Him."

Isaiah 26:3
Anchoring of redemption
Recovery of mankind
God orchestrated

I learned that God had given me a way to concentrate on something concrete--- numbers that would help me see His care for me and bring and keep me in perfect peace,

just like His
promise
spoke.

"P.J." Jefferson/ Author

Explanatory Notes

In all the languages today, different words can have the same meaning. This principle is also true in "*A Love Language from the Ageless One Through Numbers*." You will find that various numbers have the same word meaning as another number. For example, *seven* can mean *trustworthy*, but *nineteen* can also mean *trustworthy*. The number *two* can mean *solid*, but the number *seven* can also mean *solid*.

Just as there are many words to convey the particular meaning of something in English, it is the same concept in *A Love Language from the Ageless One Through Numbers'* book. He will use different words to talk with you, according to the accurate thought and meaning He knows will make the most sense for your situation.

Example: God was letting me know He was moving me into a new place in my life by using the number 40, which, in this particular situation, symbolized transition. But I also experienced a time when I had sick loved ones, where He allowed me to see the number *40*, and I knew that this transition meant passing from this life to the next. At other times when I've been ill or others with a diagnosis that held death threats, He would continuously bring my attention to the numbers that dealt with healing,' *14,'* and deliverance from my health issues, '*13.'* The number *7* can represent wholeness, totality, and completion. Or He would give me a combination of numbers, like the time read on a clock — 07:14 —which at that time was a promise of unlimited, complete, and total healing. And He has always kept His word.

I have come to understand that, like any other language, new words are continually added, and the definitions of formally known words naturally expand our understanding as we increase our knowledge. This principle has proven true over the years as God has introduced me to new words and definitions for numbers I had known by other names or meanings.

With these examples, this principle rings true because God is so vastly unlimited; I know that the words and definitions in this book are only a small sampling of what the numbers can mean. Those willing to share their experiences with this principle will hopefully encourage others to have this experience, too!

Initially, I was taught that the number *9* represented "fruitfulness." Over the years, when I encountered that number and heard the message, to my surprise, the vocabulary for that number *9* grew into a list of different meanings. Those meanings could apply to whatever was being addressed at that time. An example of this is revealed in the shortlist below.

Fruitful
Life or life-producing, lifesaving
Fertile
Future
Supply
Cultivate
Multiply

999 in one message could mean "<u>Fruitful supply for your future</u>."
999 in another number message and situation could mean "<u>Fruitful cultivation is needed to multiply</u>," whatever needs an answer on what to do.

That is why this book is formatted like a reference dictionary. It should be used at the beginning to help you understand how to use it to clarify your unique, individual conversations with God.

As with any language, there are always additions, updated words, and phrases that convey a more modern way of saying or expressing a meaning. This has never been more true than when I began recording this love language from God, which over the years expanded from the basic words and phrases I first heard in our conversations.

God is so vast, so unlimited in who He is, and the infinite wealth of knowledge we have yet to know, it only stands to reason that additional words and definitions exist, even like in a regular dictionary. There are different dictionaries in different languages from other cultures. Something can mean one thing in English and another in French, yet mean something else in German. The list goes on and on with each culture and its different languages and words.

With this being said, I know that this numbers book will open up your ears, and through your eyes, you will see what God would say to you in your language. Your awareness will be awakened, where it's not just about numbers, but those numbers will be considered unique, each one coming together to bring forth a special message for you and your life.

Because I anticipate that others will hear different words and phrases about what any particular number means in their language and culture, I invite you to share that revelation so the love language will be known to include all, not just a chosen few. When you share, you will prove that God loves talking with everyone. If you are willing to share, I would ask you to share your story about what you hear when you view different numbers. This can become an incredible cross-cultural experience we can all share.

I will be working on a revised and expanded version, and your story can be a part of that upcoming project. An email address is being provided so you can share your experience. I am excited because I know many are getting ready to have an incredible relationship with their conversations with God through numbers. I can't wait to hear from our "worldwide" listening family.

The term "timestamped promises" refers to the time or numbers displayed when the number message was revealed, which spoke to whatever was being addressed.

❖ Acronyms vs. Acrostic Style Poetry

Acronyms are not a new thing. They have been around for a long time and are used for all different kinds of things, from advertisements to the names of businesses, foundations, and schools. But most acronyms today are one or two letters for each word abbreviated.

Acronym Examples:

GE

General
Electric Company

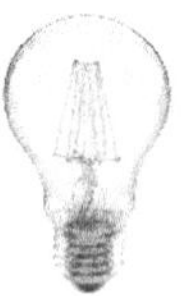

FBI
Federal
Bureau of
Investigations

ASAP
As
Soon
As
Possible

SSI
Supplemental
Security
Income

BOGO
Buy
One
Get
One

ISBN
International
Standard
Book
Number

Acrostic Style Poetry

To read acrostic-style poetry, the letters of a word are stacked beneath each other. Each letter leads to a word or words that are read as a sentence to convey the definition, description, phrase, or idea being written about, thereby increasing artistic clarity.

They simply spotlight the "depths" of what can be received as the root of "truth" in a matter. That said, the last word on a line is generally connected to the following letter line until the end of the word gives the complete thought or message.

All the letters are lined up, forming words & sentences that
Can
Really be an eye-
Opening way to
See
Things from an
Interesting point of view
Creating

Slide shows--- Show and
Tells that
You get to
Look at and
Explore the

Possibilities of anything from an
Out-of-the-box way of thinking,
Expanding
The way you think
Resulting in
Your being open to learning something new.

Just know, the Holy Spirit is the One who makes all communication possible in clarity.

❖ The Possible Peace-filled Process *for* *Learning the new form of communication from God*

In the beginning, like with learning any other language you're unfamiliar with, it's good to be prepared to go as slow as you need to and be patient with yourself. Remember, this book is intended to be a continuous source of encouragement and clarity until you and God have established your rhythm in how the language will work for your relationship. Some may quickly pick up this language and trust what has been expressed.

However, always remember that this should not be a struggle, but rather fun and comforting. And as your one-on-one communications with God grow and increase, you can use this as often as you'd like, regarding time, desire, or need. It's all up to you. God is leaving it up to you to let Him know how often or not you choose to converse with Him in this way. Don't feel bad if you're not retaining what you want or learning as fast as you would like. Don't feel rushed. This is the reason for the book, so you can refer back to it as often as you want or need. However, I would encourage you to keep a record, as your number messages begin to reflect your life's situations. In this way, you will be able to see the increase that could now lead to incredible excitement, knowing that He would choose to provide you with such a unique way to know He is present in everything that takes place in your life.

You may look for numbers at first, but later you will get a sense that He wants you to pay attention to a particular set of numbers that point to something being addressed. As you become more comfortable, you will find that He'll sometimes give you a number message to help you deal with things that haven't happened yet.

But you'll be reminded about your number message when they do, which now makes more sense. And if you're like me, you will become more profoundly in love with Him and have a greater appreciation for knowing that God is willing to address things He knew were coming, even though you didn't.

It will become as natural as breathing as you come to enjoy and depend on Him communing with you about anything in this way. Remember, one number at a time is the key to understanding and becoming fluent in "A Love Language from the Ageless One Through Numbers."

❖ Are You Open to Fresh Reveals *from God?*

Every new thing that God has released into the earth to increase us somehow has once been challenged. Some people will believe it's of the devil, something harmful until proven otherwise. Some may need scripture references to believe that God could be the author-creator who has authorized the release of this new, unlimited language for everyone who desires to commune with Him in this way. These are the scriptures He shared with me to share with you. May His Spirit bear witness with your Spirit as He invites you into greater depths of trusting that He is here waiting for you to let Him talk to you through numbers.

❖ Scriptures of Hidden Mysteries

Being revealed with "fresh revelation"

Scripture references for those who question whether or not this is of God. **Habakkuk 2:1-3**

2:1 I will stand upon my watch and watch to **see** what He will **say** to me.

2:2 And the Lord answered me and said, "Write the vision (what you saw in what He said), make it plain, record upon the **tablets**" (as well as the heart), that he may **run** who **reads** it.

Those willing to
Accept and
Believe that God
Loves
Everyone enough
To tell and
Show them He's real,

Rightly
Understanding and
Never doubting again after

Readily
Eyeballing for themselves
All that God has
Declared and
Shown them to be true and are willing to be used to bring it to pass.

2:3 For the vision is yet for an appointed time. And it hastens to the end (fulfillment); it will not deceive or disappoint. Though it tarries (appears delayed), wait for it. Because it will surely come, it will never be behind schedule on its appointed day.

1 Corinthians 2:9 Eyes hath not seen, and ears have not heard, and have not entered into the heart of man all that God has prepared, made, and keeps ready for all those who love Him.

Daniel 2:28 However, there is a God in heaven who reveals mysteries.

Daniel 2:47 Surely your God is a God of gods and a Lord of kings and a revealer of mysteries since you have been able to reveal this mystery.

Job 12:22 He reveals mysteries from the darkness and brings the deep darkness into the light.

Daniel 2:22 It is He who reveals the profound and hidden things. He knows what is in the darkness, and the light dwells with Him.

Jeremiah 33:3 Call to Me, and I will answer you and tell you great and mighty things you do not know.

Daniel 2:30 But as for me, this mystery has not been revealed to me for any wisdom residing in me more than any other living man, but to make the interpretation known to me and that you may understand the thoughts of your mind.

Ephesians 1:9 Having made known to us the mystery of His will, according to His good pleasure, which He purposed in Himself.

Ephesians 3:3 The mystery was made known to me by revelation.

❖ Because He Cares About Your Knowing

How detailed and intentional His thoughts are toward you

Jeremiah 29:11 For I know the thoughts and plans I have for you, says the Lord. Thoughts and plans for welfare (good) and peace, and not for evil. To give you hope in your final outcome.

Psalms 139: 17-18

17: How precious and weighty are Your thoughts to me, Oh God! How vast is the sum of them?

18: If I could count them, they would be more in number than the grains of sand.

Psalms 40:5 Many, Oh Lord, my God, are the wonderful works You have done, and Your thoughts toward us; no one can compare with You! They are too many to be numbered if I should declare and speak of them.

❖ God---The Original Author and Definer of "Words"

What God uses to
Openly show the
Range of His power when He
Demonstratively
Spoke the world into existence, allowing His Spirit time to reveal the awesomely unlimited vast heights, lengths, widths, and depths of all of what He created with His power-filled words.

We are created in God's image and likeness and have the same power to create with our words. God's power is in your mouth, your "**tongue**."

Tool of communication that is
Often used in
Not so good ways that negatively
Give power to things we don't want, not
Understanding how
Endowed we are to do good for everyone with our words and corresponding actions that can change our world for the better.

He who has given man, by His Spirit, the ability to define with words and create just like Him, taught me what words went to which number and the definition if there were new ways to see the word.

At other times, I was given the okay to use the descriptions He had already provided by those He allowed to write dictionaries. I always want to let the reader know who the source is that is providing the resources.

God and I do not want anyone to miss out on this exciting time of a "fresh" new way to communicate. It is a more direct form of communication than technology, because God gave us the ability to develop technology for our use. Let's start to desire to converse with "The Source" more than depending on "the resources." So know, God is...

Supreme
Overall, when it comes to
Understanding the
Right way to
Communicate with
Each and every one of us

Release of
Everything from "The Source" to
Supplement what's needed to
Overcome obstacles that would
Undermine the
Release and reveal of things
Coming into
Existence that's needed to
thrive and
Survive

If a Merriam-Webster's Dictionary was used as a reference, the word would be preceded by this symbol *****, for *The Oxford English Dictionary*, this symbol ⌖, and for the *Encyclopedia Britannica*, this symbol ✠. The King James and the Amplified versions of the Holy Bible have been used as references in this book.

So, Dear Reader,

This book has been written so that you, too, can find peace and loving assurance, learning to know how much He personally cares for you.

I wish you *sweet communications* for the enrichment of your life.

This book is

Directional,

Instructional,

Inspirational,

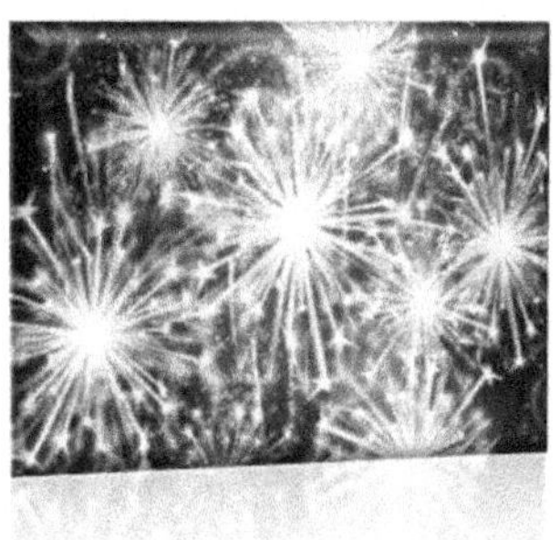

as well as ***FUN*** !!!

Building a legacy of ***Faith***

The finding of ***Forever Love***

Evelyn P.J. Jefferson

The Ageless One Defined

Ancient has always been

God The

Eternal (forever will be)

Lover of

Everyone, who is ready to

Save all by

Showing us who we really are;

Omnies made in His image

Needing nothing extra but to fully

Embrace all that He is within us.

Absolutely
"All Things Work"
When You Trust in <u>God</u>

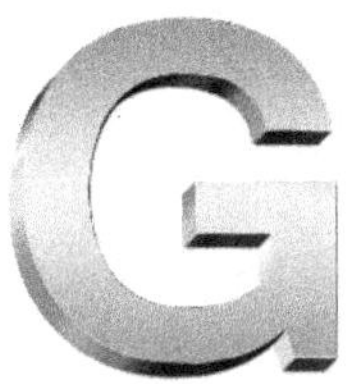

REAT generous, gentle maker/creator of all things, universes, galaxies, and then there would be You and me

mnipotent (All-Powerful)

mniscient (All-Knowing)

mnipresent (Everywhere at the same time)

over everything, but most importantly, He is "head over heels" in LOVE with you and me.

ivine deity who desired and decided to ownload Himself into you and me for His good pleasure of having His children made in His image to enjoy all He has made. So, we who are creators just like our "Father" in Heaven could do the same... make new creations of things for our good pleasure.

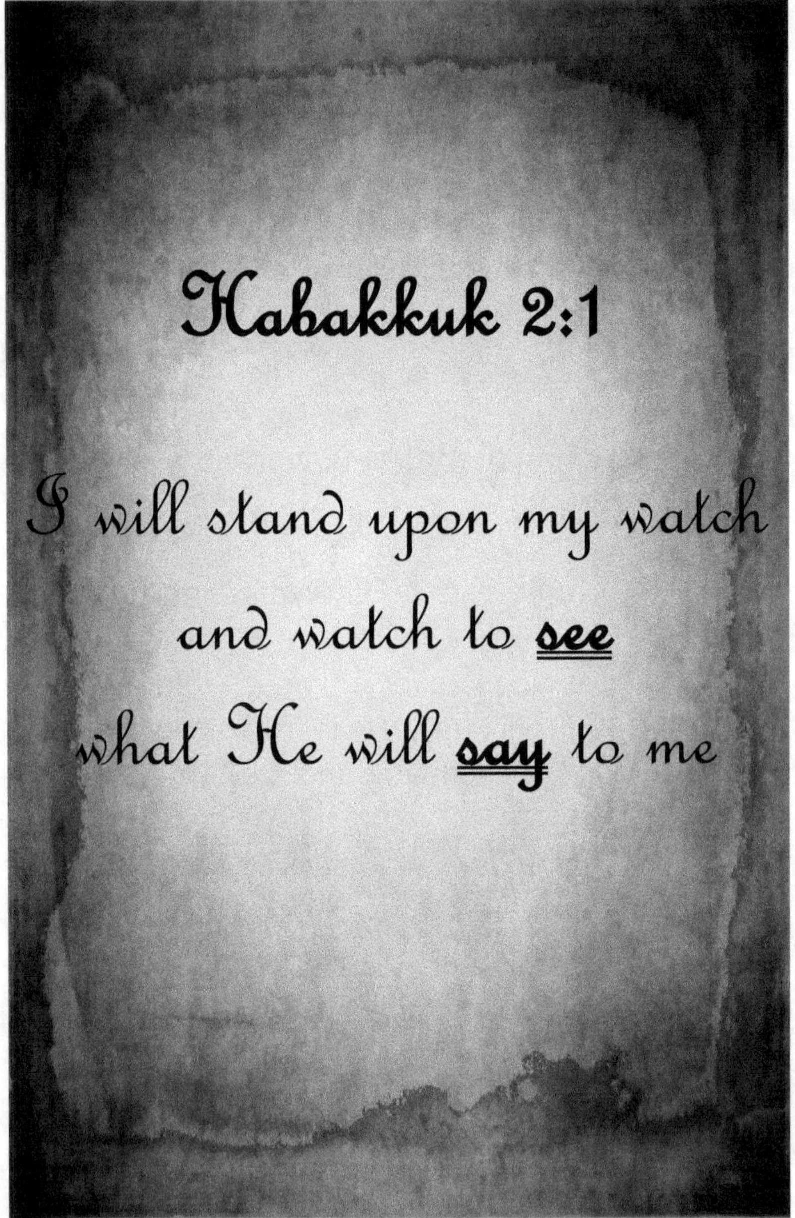
Habakkuk 2:1
I will stand upon my watch
and watch to see
what He will say to me

I Will STAND on My WATCH and SEE What the Lord Will SAY to Me

Stay still.
Take time to
Acknowledge the
Need to
Daringly,

Wherever I Am,
Ask for
Truth so I
Can
Hear the

Soundness of what our
Eternal
Everlasting Father would say,

So, I can
Agree and give my
Yes, to His will for my life.

LISTEN

Matthew 11:15 *"He who has ears to hear, let him be listening and let him consider and perceive and comprehend by hearing."*

God is speaking. He is speaking all the time through many different things, ways; and, yes, people.
The only real criteria for hearing Him is your having a desire to
Listen.

Letting
In the
Sound of His voice without
Trying to
Erase or alter what's
Not pleasing or
acceptable
by your now
measurements
of who you
think He is, but being open to Him revealing
the truth of who He is

INTRODUCTION

How exciting would it be if there were a way to know God's heart of love and care for you anytime, day or night, without having to trust in a third party, such as priests, ministers, psychic readers, family, friends, or internet contexts, as if they were God, through something as simple as numbers? Although God has given us each other to help encourage, speak words of wisdom, and pray for and with each other, those things and people were never designed to replace Him. We were designed to move with Him, for Him, but never replace Him in our dependency on Him. Regardless of our trusting someone else's connection to God, we were not meant to depend on it.

But you can have an open "one-to-one" relationship with He who made you. God knows everything about you and is waiting to lovingly encourage and empower you to live a more fearless and "on purpose-filled life" where you and God have the final say regarding anything that could be relevant to you.

Regardless of how God has made you, there are different ways and communications that could be a more natural fit for you to feel one with Him. Each place, situation, and use of gifts and talents could make you feel closer to the One who created you.

Just as uniquely different as we all are, in this book, God wants to let you know that you can have a universal way to communicate with Him one-on-one and moment-by-moment through something as simple as numbers.

A visual presentation of different revelations through acrostic-style poetry in *A Love Language from the Ageless One Through Numbers* is included.

This book is for anyone who has ever wondered whether or not "The God of the Universes" knows or cares about them. Even for those who know Him but are doubtful and unsure when they start to journey through harsh, hard times, sometimes with no good ending in sight, you, too, can benefit.

I want to share how you can know the "Heavenly Father's heart" towards you every moment. This includes situations with people, family, friends, businesses, ministries, etc., but especially those things you can't share with anyone that are found deep in your heart. It's okay because He knows all and sees all. And He is waiting to share with you how to view unlimited possibilities for your present-day situations, including the comfort and assurance of knowing nothing has been by chance. All things have a purpose, and you can experience these amazing one-on-one conversations through this book that God has provided for anyone who desires to converse with Him in this way.

I have come to depend on and appreciate the consistent faithfulness of having God reaffirming He was there and working things out while going through some of the craziest, hellish, hard times I've ever lived. Through everyday numbers, times, dates, bill invoices, street signs, ID numbers, telephone numbers, and more, God's confirming messages spoke of Him being there amid it all. That empowered me to know that I had a brighter future if I kept embracing the messages of peace throughout my day until things worked out. He always knew what I needed and how often I needed to see and know. He spoke to my situation, sometimes minute by minute, moment by moment, confirming He was there. His thoughts and plans for my good helped me hold on to hope until those more incredible things could manifest in His perfect timing.

Some of those experiences were life-and-death regarding health issues, relationships, money matters, and so much more. So, with these things in mind, this book is written so others can experience the same peace, joy, and excitement of knowing God's thoughts and plans for good for their "right now" situation and their future, at any time, day or night.

This is different from astrology, which deals with the dependence of how the stars align to give you any sense of things in life that life was a “by chance” kind of thing. These number messages are from the One who spoke the stars and planets into being—the same One who created you on purpose. You matter. Even science defines you as “matter,” the subject of which a physical object is composed. The dictionary describes you like this: *A subject of interest or concern to be influential; An indefinite amount or quantity (unlimited) "to be of importance."* You are on purpose, and God is ready to speak to you and prove it.

The information provided is not about learning how to have everything go your way all the time magically, but this book will reveal the truth that God is real. He cares and wants you to know He's ready and willing to help you in your everyday life, not just on occasions of desperate prayers, but He's waiting to tell you that with what's found in this book, how every day, without religious rituals, you and He can have a friendship that is

Unshakable,
Unbreakable,
Enjoyable and
Powerful for the rest of your life.

Ezekiel 3:10 Moreover, He said to me, "Son of man (daughter) receive into your heart all my words which I speak to you and hear with your ears."

Listen Closely.

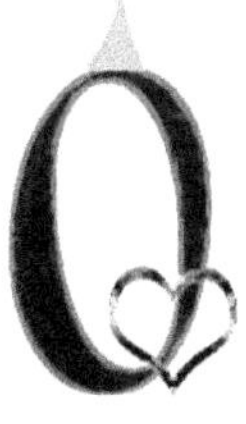

0/Zero

Zenith (highest)

Entity

Regarding

Ongoing forever possibilities

Sometimes, the misunderstood "Unsung" hero of the number system, we've been taught conventionally that "zero" holds no real value unless attached to another number. This chapter on number zero will help you change your mindset. In God's *Love Language from the Ageless One Through Numbers,* zero represents the awesome, unlimitedness of God toward you and all of what life could hold for you.

Zero, The "Wild Card" of Our Number Language

The Unknown Variable: A component always ready to be used as a "**wild card**."

Whatever
Is needed to help
Level the playing field,
Determine the outcome

Causing
Anything to be possible
Regarding what is a
Doubtful situation now made "doable"

Power

Propelling
Onward
Wind from within that
Everyone has, but some have a problem
Recognizing and using it to enrich their own and others' lives

Unlimited: Without limits or restrictions

Uttermost: (highest elevation) It goes on and on and on through an upward position, reminding us that anything is possible. The extent of God's good and great thoughts toward us cannot be satisfied with our limited ability to think or imagine.

Infinite: Goes on and on and on and on forever, not governed by time

Vast: (Very significant in size) Without borders

Unbelievable: (Except by faith) Things that can take place that you've never heard or seen before, making it hard for you to believe what God is showing or allowing to be heard.

Endless Possibilities

Immeasurable: Cannot be measured, counted, or viewed all at once

Unfathomable: (Depths of "the unknown") too deep to be fully understood

Utterly Unmatched: No comparison can be made

Omnipotent: Having unlimited authority and power

Omnipresent: Present in all places at the same time

Omniscient: All-Knowing

Out of the Box Thinking: It is not like the typical thinking process, but is seen in ways that may not make sense to others' way of understanding.

Absolutely No Boundaries, Limitless: Without any restrictions whatsoever. As far as the "imagination" can go, then continuous continuance.

***Over:** **1.** Across a barrier or intervening space
2. Across a brim
3. To bring the underside up (to flip)
4. Beyond some quantity, limit, or norm
5. All through, thoroughly
6. Upper, higher
7. Above in position, authority, or scope
8. To exceed or surpass
9. Remaining

Ultimate: Nothing can top it

Undeniable: Impossible to deny

Unheard of: Unprecedented, never heard of before or previously known

Unconditional: Absolutely no requirements or conditions to qualify for

Overcomer/Overcoming: Victorious conqueror (ing)

Overseeing: Look after, watch over

***Exponential:** The multiplying factor characterized by an extremely rapid increase (as in size or extent)

Open-Ended while being All-Inclusive: Open for more while being protective of the already present whole

Generous: This term deals with being open-hearted and gracious.

Super Abundance: Extreme; more than enough; unlimited abundance

Increase: Addition and multiplication

***Elevate:** To lift, raise, exalt, elate (to fill with joy)

***Elevation:** A lifting up

***Conquer:** To get the better of, overcome, defeat

Forever: A time with no end

Beyond Measure

More Than Enough

Overflow

1/One

Original intent for the

Natural

Existence of God, man, and all living things

✠**Single-minded:** Having only one purpose, goal, or interest, focused on one thing.

The power of one --- the power of **you**. The God of all creation saw fit to create you; one created in His image, awesomely unlimited, powerful, and creative. He graces you to be just like Him if you want to be. Ask Him to reveal Himself to you so you can be introduced to "the real **You**."

Now, if zero represents God's unlimitedness, how awesome is it to know that in and with Him "alone," as ONE, we cannot be measured by any "earthly" anything?

The mind struggles to understand this because there are few or no points of reference that could begin to explain what only the Spirit of man, from the Spirit of God, could ever know to be true.

1 Cor. 2:14 says that no man can know things unless by God's Spirit, Spirit to Spirit, and not head-to-head.

We are all "awesome," but not all of us know it. Be open for God to reveal this truth to you on an ongoing basis —literally a forever "discovery" — until you, who have agreed for Papa God to be your loving father, return home to heaven.

Know that we come from the heart of God. We are spirits dwelling in flesh and bone (earth-suits). But, when our time to transition from earth into eternity comes, those who have made it known their desire to live out eternity with God will now receive a "Nu" body, a "**glorified body**," a God-designed body, perfected to live in the "perfect."

God has
Lovingly crafted
Overcoats for the
Royals to
Identify with as the
Fresh coat of
Invincibility to
Evil
Disease that

Bothered us while we were here
On earth, causing all kinds of
Distressing doubt regarding our true God-image identity, which
led us to
Yield to lies about who we were and who we could be.

Oneness (State of being): Intentional openness of heart "agreement"

Unity: The state or description of those who practice oneness

All: Fully Inclusive

***Balance (d):** A state of equilibrium; an amount of excess on a credit side of an account; to arrange so that one set of elements is equal to another; to bring into harmony or proportion

One of a Kind: Not another one like it

Unique: Unlike anything else; having no like or equal; one of a kind; unparalleled; very unusual

✞**Uniqueness:** The quality of being only one of this kind; the quality of being particularly remarkable, exceptional, or unusual

Union: (Intimate) Coming together to make one intimately, such as in marriage

Commitment

***Rarity, Oddity:** Excellent, wonder-filled, splendid; more than what was mentioned, in addition to what is usual; unfamiliar, new

Strange, Peculiar: Far from the ordinary, not easily understood

Equal: Equivalent, evenly balanced, level

Uni: Nickname of us as individuals; a unit of uniqueness

Unit: The smallest number representative of God's unlimitedness.

Everyone and Everything

I
Me
You
She
He
Him
Her
They
Those
Us
Our
These
Them

A
The
It
This
That
Every
Only
Particular (ly)
In-between

These **sight** words you could hear in your conversation with God for this number.

Specified or singled out as to which
Individual (s) or
Groups or things
Having
The main "subject" placement in your conversation with God

Essential to help with journaling

2/Two

The

Word form of the number that describes

Our being set apart, distinctively having the ability to reason and act with God's gift of free will to use as we choose.

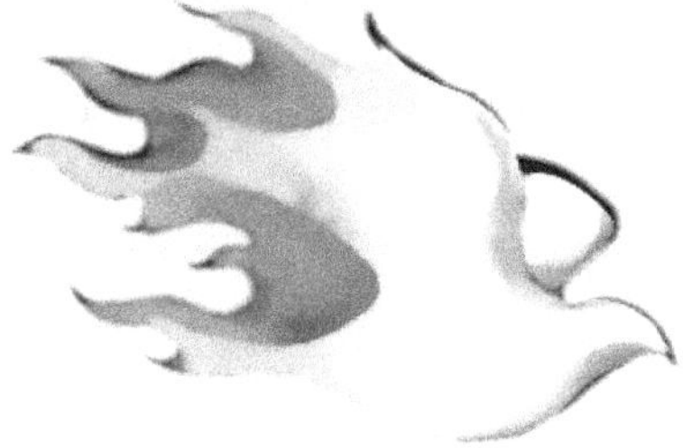

***Rise:** Ascend; to increase in quantity or intensity; to come into "Being" to return from death.

Reach
Inside.
Set your
Expectations for elevations, then follow through with God's help.

Holy: Sacred

Highest
Observance of
Love
You can yield to,
to love and receive

High
On
Loving
You

Highest caliber of
honesty that
Only
Love can provide
for us to
Yield to

✞**Sacred:** Regarded with great respect and reverence

Set Apart: To be intentionally separated for a specific purpose

Sanctify (ied, ing): Consecrate; purify; blessed dedication

Sacrifice: Something done at a cost

Sacrificial: A selfless act of sacrificing, giving up something of value on behalf of others.

Consecrate (ed, tion, ing): To make or declare as sacred; to devote seriously (soberly) to a purpose

Anoint (ed, ing): To bless; to set apart; to consecrate

***Sanction:** Authoritative approval

Honor: Outward respect and reverence, or to pay homage to

Distinct: Presenting a clear and unmistakable impression

***Surprising:** Unexpected or amazing to cause astonishment

***Radical:** Very different from the usual or traditional; extreme; favoring extreme changes in existing views, habits, conditions, or institutions; A group of **atoms** considered as a unit that remains unchanged during reactions

Readiness to
Altar
Drastically
If need be,
Currently
Accepted norms that no
Longer addresses the needs of right now or future challenges

Are
Those who are
Open to
Major changes
Suddenly, without being rattled

🕈**Reset:** To start again after a period of rest or change; to start something over again or adjust it; to set, adjust, or fix something in a new or different way

***Reserve (ed):** To store for future or specific use

***Stabilize (ed):** To hold steady

***Balance (ed):** A state of equilibrium to bring into harmony or proportions

☦Solidify: Make stronger; reinforce

Send Off

Sanctioning an agreement to the
Ending of something with encouragement for the
Next step in the journey
Displaying an

Overwhelming, overcoming
Faith for a
Fruitful future for everyone involved

Depart

Decision to leave a place or situation
Even if
Parting ways
Appears to be
Running from hardship and hurt when in
Truth, it can be a "time" of increase for all involved

"Spot" Me Please

See my need looking
Pass my
Offensive
Tendencies and "help me please"

Support: To assist; to hold up or serve as a foundation

***Complement:** To add to, to come alongside, to fill up or fill out; to make someone complete or whole

***Guard:** A defensive position; The act or duty of protecting or defending; To watch over

***Collaborate:** To work jointly with others

***Sustain (s, ed):** To keep going; to hold up; endure

✝Cover (s): Taking up a position ready to defend what's oppressively opposing

Committing to
Oppose
Various
Evils on behalf of the oppressed,
Remaining dependably in place
Steadfastly, regardless of being faced with enticing compromises

***Second:** Alternate; One who assists another; To encourage or give support to

Someone who is supportive and
Equipped to
Come into an agreement to be
On-call if a
Need arises that
Denotes a need for continuous structure or leadership
"back-up"

Reinforce: An additional layer of strength and/or protection.

Wait: To remain still but in readiness with expectation to hear or think about what to do next.

Willingness to
Accept that
In
Time, things will come together and be *worked out* without you trying to make it happen.

Schedule: Timetable to appoint, assign, or designate for a fixed time

***Second:** The 60th part of a minute of time or angular measure

Small section of time that
Exist to help us
Command
Ourselves to
Not be
Deceived about how important "The Gift of Time" is for us on earth

***Resolute (ion):** Firmly determined in purpose

***Anchor:** To hold or become held in place; to be a stabilizing force for foundation

***Solid:** Thoroughly dependable and reliable; serious in purpose or character

Cement: To unite, reinforce, fortify; to bring together

***Bond (ed, able):** A binding or uniting force or tie (like, as in friendship); an agreement or obligation made binding by a pledge; to become firmly united as if by bonds

Twosome: Two in unity

***Predestined:** Set Time; to settle beforehand; foreordained

Sent from
Eternity, an assigned increment of
Time

That
Is
Meant to
Establish and tell the story of the intentionality of the plans and promises of God. Everything has a "timer on it." Nothing is by chance or happenstance.

***Awaits:** wait for; expect

A timed opportunity, adventure, or encounter that is
Waiting to be
Accessed by the arrival of the
Individual (s)
That
Seek to experience such things

Author's Note: Always remember, God does not treat us like puppets. He gave us *free will.* So God's intentionality and our free will choices set the time for anything we encounter.

Promise (d): Pledge, confirmed vow

***Seal (ed):** Guarantee, pledge, authenticate; to close or make secure against access, leakage, or passage; to determine irrevocably

Rhythm and Rhyme

Refers to
Having a
Yes
Tempo of
Harmony with someone
Making it

Absolutely a
No-brainer when
Decisions need to be made that

Respect is the
Harmonizing factor
Yielding
More than
Enough to succeed at whatever needs to be achieved

***Tight:** Strongly fixed or held; secure; set close together; close; intoxicated

High
On
Loving
You

Tight in relationship with God is;

Together
In such an intimate way that
Gives no opening for
Heart
Tampering to interrupt the connection

The "Tenor and Tone" ...the sound, color, and feel of an
Intimate relationship with
God, giving
Him the highest placement in your heart
To solidify a forever oneness from knowing that's where you are in His heart

Scripture: 1 John 4:19; *We love because He first loved us.*

***Assure:** To give confidence to; to state confidently to make certain the coming or the attainment of

***Assurance:** Pledge: security: self-confidence: Audacity (a willingness to take bold risks)

Secure: (Tucked or squirreled away, sometimes hidden in plain sight) To make safe; to guard, shelter, protect; to make confident

***Sequester (ed):** Set apart; segregate (for safety purposes); to deliberate and deliver intent without distractions or interference

***Secure (ed):** Easy in mind; free from fear; free from danger or risk of loss; made to feel safe.

Security: Reassurance; safety; refuge; safe haven

Held in Trust

Holding back of
Everything of value that could be squandered (wasted) &
Lend to your
Downfall

If released before maturity, could
Naturally, prepare you

To know how to handle or even
Regard or
Understand the
Stewardship your
Trust funds require what these valuables were
meant for

***Secretly:** Kept from general knowledge

Secluded, squirreled away until the
Eventual need
Comes about that
Requires an
Emergence or the
True nature of a matter be revealed so that
Lies are not
Yielded to as "Truth"

***Segment (ed, ation, ing):** Section; a division of a thing

Divide (ed, sive, sion): Separate; segment (cut up or off from the whole); disunity

***Segregate (ed, ing, ion):** To cut off from others

***Disunity:** Lack of unity, dissension

***Demote:** To reduce; to lower grade or rank

***Reject (ed, ion):** To refuse to accept, consider, use, or submit to

Refused
Entrance into personal or group situations
Justified at times by those with an
Elitist point of view
Causing
Those who are followers to
Incite
Oppressive behavior,
Negative and disrespectful

***Split:** To divide into parts or sections

Decrease: To grow or cause to grow less; diminish; reduction

3/Three

The

Host of heaven

Ready to

Explain and show a picture of how

Eternity is here on earth

Papa loves showing up in threes:

Father	Body
Son	Soul
Holy Spirit	Spirit

God to Man
Man to God
Man to each other

God Working in 3s

Father Son Holy Spirit	{ }	Omnipotent Omniscient Omnipresent
3 Body 2 Soul 1 Spirit	{ }	1 Spirit 2 Soul 3 Body
Outer Court Inner Court Holy of Holies	{ }	Biblically Parts of the Tabernacle for the Children of Israel

Trimesters in pregnancy are counted in 3s

1st Trimester
2nd Trimester
3rd Trimester

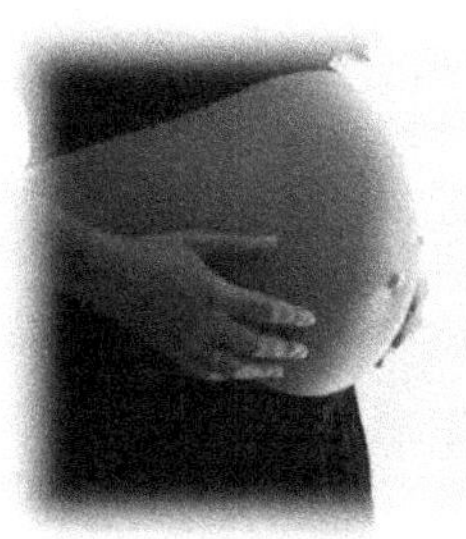

The Atom =

Protons
Neutrons
Electrons

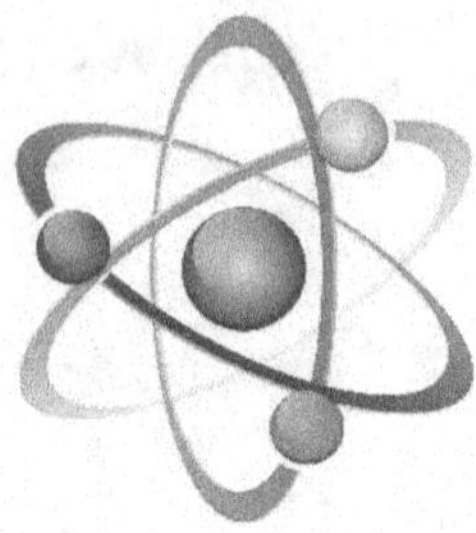

Personality =

ID
Superego
Ego

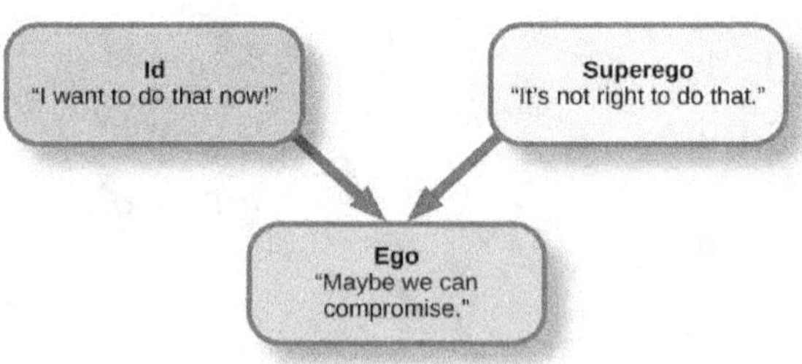

Earth =

Crust
Mantle
Core

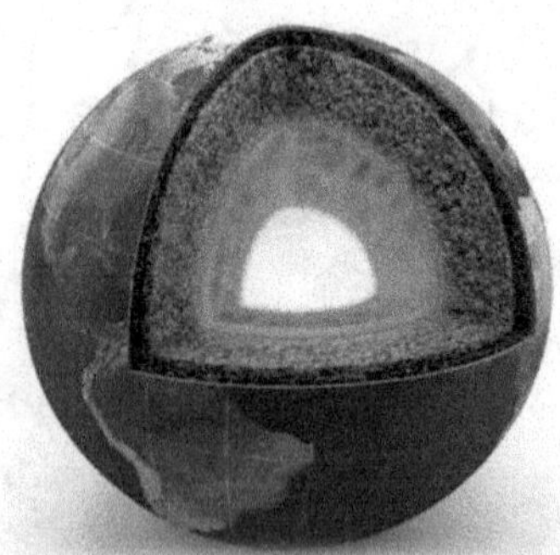

Healthy Relationships

Ecclesiastes 4:12B A threefold cord is not easily broken.

A threefold cord is not easily broken. The third person of the Godhead, the Holy Spirit, is here to strengthen, reinforce, and bind those who want to be bound together.

Marriages

Parents and Children

Friendships

This truth prevails if God, who is love, is in the relationship.

God: The Almighty Creator, He who has no beginning and no end, He who is Omnipotent (All-Powerful)
Omniscient (All-Knowing)
Omnipresent (Everywhere at the same time)

God --- Father, Son, Holy Spirit

He who is loving, kind, caring, holy, and the highest form of righteousness

Righteous (ness): Acting or being in accordance with what is just, honorable, and free from guilt or wrong. Syn., virtuous, noble, moral, ethical, HOLY

***Power:** Authority; one who has control or authority; force or energy used to do; dominion

Resurrection Power: The ability to bring dead things back to life, regardless of how long they've been dead

Retroactive Power: Ability to reset and restore things in such a fantastic way that it would seem as if it had always been that way (like there was never an interruption in the state of a thing)

Retribution on The Spirit of Death: Revenge, vengeance, or retaliation on death, by the raising to life through resurrection power.

Breath is God: Spoken sound of His Spirit; air inhaled or exhaled in breathing

Breath is Life!!!

Empower (ed, ment): The release of power from one source to another

Raised from Obscurity: Things or people that have been hidden are now brought forth to be seen

Divine (Divinity): The nature and state of being on a higher plane with God and all His attributes, greater than human existence

***Mystery:** A known religious truth by revelation alone; something difficult or impossible to understand or explain

Miracle and Miraculous: Things that happen outside the scope of what man has said could or could not take place; things that prove nothing is impossible and God is real.

Supernatural: That which can transcend beyond natural laws of "**science**."

Set
Calculated
Information that speaks to say only the
Educated, experienced in known
Natural laws,
Could
Ever be what's possible

Erasable Without a Trace: Situations so resolved with/by the grace of God, only those who knew it took place could have ever believed that something had ever happened

Example (s):

Broken relations, addictions, financial ruin, mental illness, homelessness, and illnesses of all kinds can be so healed and mended that only those who were part of the process could believe the restoration (as if nothing ever happened)

Real, Reality, Realized, Realization: Nothing false, fabricated, faked, or omitted (the whole truth)

***Retro-Fit:** To furnish with newly available equipment

Retroactive: (especially of legislation) Taking effect from a date in the past; to put things right from previous decrees that had not been honored to have things be as if there had never been anything else.

Eternity: The place that is not governed by time.

Heaven

Headquarters for
Every
Authorized being with
Various assignments to
Exist in loving peace until
Needed appearances are commanded by God, requested by man for designated purposes in the earth

Home of harmonious
Eternal (forever)
Adoration displayed in
Various forms of worship by
Everything and everyone who
Now resides there

Home to the
Eternal God
And all the
Various
Entities (angels, people, and other numerous creations)
Now and forevermore, have agreed to live in the peace of the Love of God

***Energy:** Usable power

Accelerate (ion): To speed up; to bring about quicker

God Orchestrated: God's providential, perfectly precision-timed reveal of His involvement.

***God Inspired:** To influence, move, or guide by divine or supernatural inspiration

God Honoring: Respectful and worshipful thing to be, say, or do for Him

God Granted: His consent to allow; a gift given for a particular purpose

God Sculpted: Tailor-made by Him

God Crafted

Great
Omnipotent, omniscient, omnipresent
Divine essence of life deciding to design and

Create in a
Really
Artistic way that
Frames the
Truth that
Everything He does is
Done on purpose. He leaves nothing to chance.

God Designed: His deliberate arrangement of details for a particular outcome

God Explained: Only God can explain it.

God Available: What's accessible that He provided

***Strength:** The quality of being strong; ability to do or endure power, intensity; power to resist attack

***Spiritual:** Relating to or consisting of affecting the spirit

***Spirit:** Breath; a life-giving force

4/Four

Following

Our

Unique

Right to create just like our "creator," God

Will

Womb of
Intent
Longing to be
Laid to rest in fulfillment

***Create:** To bring into being

***Creator:** The One who creates

Creation: What is made or brought into existence

Creative: The unique way involving the imagination or original ideas, especially the production of artistic work

Creativity: The ability to transcend traditional ideas, rules, patterns, and relationships to create meaningful new ideas, forms, methods, interpretations, progressiveness, or imagination

***Need:** A condition requiring supply or relief.

Necessity is the Search-
Engine that
Encourages and
Draws out "creativity"

***Solution:** An action or process of solving a problem; an answer to a problem

Seeker
Of
Leveling
Understanding
To
Initiate
Overcoming ways to meet and solve
Needs

***Plan (ned, ing):** A method for accomplishing an objective

Perfecting preparations
Long before
Actions are taken to
Now bring something into a manifested state of

***Thing:** A matter of concern; state of affairs; event; circumstances; deed; act of distinct entity; an inanimate object distinguished from a living being; possessions; effects; an article of clothing; detail; point; idea or notion; something one likes to do

The
Happening
In this instance, that
Needs to be
Given attention to

The
Housing of
Ideas, intents, situations, or objects
Needing a
God revealed and sometimes answers for

***Provide:** To see ahead; to take measures beforehand; to supply what's needed; to equip

***Matter:** A subject of interest or concern: to be of importance: the substance of which a physical object is composed: an indefinite amount or quantity.

Procreate (tion): To be a part of a transfer from the heart of God into the earth, bringing forth New Life * To bring forth offspring

♰**Being:** Existence; nature or essence of a person

Being: The state of a behavior, ex. You're being mean.

Bring forth an
Embodiment of our Creator God
Involving the multifaceted sides of Him,
Nature and all living things
Growing and "becoming" miraculous displays of change

Life: An Extension of heaven
Love in the **form** of the natural and spiritual **essence** of God's heart. * The existence of being (proof of matter and movement)

Nature: The beginning and the essence of a person or thing; natural God-made scenery and environment

***Grow (ing)**: To spring up and develop into maturity

***Move (ment):** To change or cause to change positions; to go from one point to another; to show marked activity; to take action; a calculated step to achieve an objective.

Growth: A result or product of growing

***Continue:** To maintain without interruption; endure; last; to remain in place or condition; extend; to persist in

***Positive (ly, ity):** Affirmative, as in favorable, as in confident, as in conclusive or certain

Position to
Observe
Situations from an
Intrinsically
Truthful and
Insightful
Viewpoint that
Encourages a problem-solving, winning attitude for successful outcomes

***Produce:** To give birth to, give rise to, or bring about

"Work the Plan"
Focus on Follow-through
Recipe for Success

***Manifest (ation)**: To make evident or certain by showing or displaying

***Nurture:** Training, upbringing; the influence that modifies the expression of an individual's heredity

***Train:** To cause to grow as desired; to form by instruction, discipline, or drill; to make or become prepared (as by exercise) for a test or skill; to aim or point at an object.

***Nourish (ed, ing, ment):** To promote the growth or development of

Increase: Addition; expansion

***Learn (ed, Ing):** To gain knowledge, understanding, or skill by study or experience

Cultivate: To do what is necessary to continue the growth process; to weed, seed, water, prune
(Cut, sever, let go of dead things)

Build: To construct

***Groundbreaking:** Introducing new ideas or methods.

***Form:** Shape structure; the essential nature of a thing; established manner of doing or saying something; to train, instruct, compose, develop

To Use: To put into action or service

***Make/Made:** To prepare, set in order, appoint, enact, execute; to conclude, to construct

***Process:** A series of actions or operations directed toward a particular result; proceeding; progress, advance

***Way:** Road, path, route; a course of action; possible course method; individual characteristic or peculiarity; something having direction, state, or condition.

What is
Appropriate contemplative thought or action that
You should consider and do to be in the best place possible

***Work:** Toil, labor, and energy used when a force is applied over a given distance: To solve by reasoning or calculation; To exert oneself physically or mentally; To make way, slowly with difficulty; To try to influence or persuade.

Work
Without Including God

Worry and an
Overwhelming sense of
Really not achieving much with not
Knowing God honors the best you can do as more than enough without "killing" yourself to prove what you're worth

Including God

Worry-free
Opportunity to
Rely on God to
Keep you, as you display what excellence looks like as you do the best that you can

***Called:** To be acknowledged, invited, summoned; to announce authoritatively; brought forth to be established in a particular position

Care (d) for: Watchful attention; to be concerned over; to feel responsible for

☩Touch: Come into contact with; a small amount; a trace

***Touch:** To come close; to move to sympathetic feelings; to affect the interest of; concern

Touch: To make a difference

To be
Open to
Understand true
Caring, most times, takes a
Hands-on approach to be believed (No touch is Insignificant.)

Change: To make or become different

***Transform:** To change in structure, appearance, or character

Collaborate (tion): Coming together, joining creative ideas, methods, talents, and skills to bring something into manifestation

***Incorporate:** To unite closely to form one body; blend; to give material form to; to embody

***Participate (ion):** To take part in something; share

Connect (ed, ion): Join – link, bond

***Capability:** Having the ability, capacity, or power to do something; able, competent

***Intervention (s):** The act of interfering with the outcome or course, especially of a condition or process, to prevent harm or improve functioning.

Design: Blueprints, written plans, or sketched picture plans to go before something is made.

Invest: To give of oneself or/and resources to ensure the success of someone or something.

Rate and Speed: Quality, as well as time spent creating anything.

***Productivity:** The quality, state, act, or fact of being able to generate, create, enhance, or bring forth; is a measure of the efficiency of a person completing a task; is getting important things done consistently.

***Perform (ance):** Fulfill; carry out, do; function; to do in a set manner.

***Able:** Having sufficient power, skill, or resources to accomplish an objective.

***Ability:** The quality of being able; power, skill, capacity, fitness, or tendency to act or be acted on in a specific way.

Measurable: To count the whole of creating, "especially the effort," will encourage the finish.

***Excavate:** To hollow out; to dig out and remove earth; to form by hollowing out (expose, remove, and make room); to reveal; to view by digging away at the covering.

Spiritual Application

Decide to
Invest in
Going beyond being

Defined by someone
Else's understanding of what's just
Enough to stay
Part of "The Status Quo"

Deciding to
Intentionally
Go beyond the

Depth of
Easy accessibility of anything and
Enter into being
Prepared to press to know,
Expose and explore the
Root of a matter

Grounded: Firmly established, natural, and sincere

Genuine and
Real when being
Open to
Understand what's
Needed to
Differentiate between what's
Evil or what's good
Drawing lines of "demarcation" to live by

***Fix:** To make firm, stable or fast; to give a permanent or final form to; to hold or direct steadily; establish, set; assign; to set in order; adjust; to prepare; to make whole or sound again; an accurate determination or understanding

***Minister:** To give aid or service

Meant to be an
Investment of
Nurturing, showing how God
Is interested in
Seeing to your needs
Through someone's willingness to
Earnestly
Reveal God's heart through service

Business: A need-meeter that generates income.

***Serve:** to be of use

***Service:** The act, fact, or means of serving; performance of an official and professional duty.

***Career:** An occupation or profession followed as a life's work

✟**Raise Up:** To change the arrangement or position of something; to awaken, arouse, or stir; put on a higher level; to place higher in rank or dignity.

Lift up --- Elevate

***Initiate:** To start; to begin something; to be proactive (make things happen instead of waiting for them to happen)

***Operate:** To perform work; to function; to produce effort; to put or keep in operation

***Promote (ion):** To advance in station, rank, or honor; to contribute to the growth or prosperity of; to launch

***Maintain:** To keep an existing state (as of repair); to sustain against opposition or danger; to continue in; to carry on; to provide for; support

***Diligence:** Characterized by steady, earnest, energetic effort; painstaking

***Progression:** An act of progressing; advance; a continuous and connected series of movement

***Go:** To undertake; to give wholehearted support; surpass; energy, vigor; functioning properly

GO

Get going
Onward

How

Having an
Obvious
Way of doing something that, after being seen or instructed, can be reproduced

Done

Denoted to having
Officially come to a point where
Nothing
Else is needed to be considered finished

"Just Do It!"

Step out.

Go forward.

Make A Difference

However You Can

With

Whatever You Have

5/Five

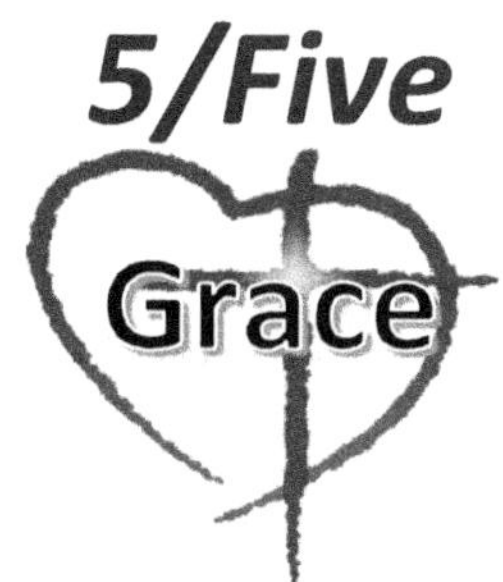

Faith in God

Invested in a

Very "vital" way so

Eternity can be embraced and
experienced by mankind on the earth

***Grace:** Unmerited (Can't earn it. It's not for sale); help given to people by God (as in overcoming temptation).

Grace

God-given

Resources

Accessed by

Calling out to Him, believing and knowing His

Ears miss nothing (especially where we are concerned)
even when it doesn't seem like it.

Glimpses of God's heart
Ready to
Assist us when we
Call on Him,
Especially when we depend on Him only

Governing power from heaven that
Regulates and empowers
All our
Choices to do right by
Everyone (It is God who makes that possible.)

Grants permission
Regarding how
Anyone
Chooses to live,
Even during the times you're learning what's best.

Greatest gift of love needed
Regarding
Anything that we
Could
Ever be granted for living a successful life ---
The miraculous power of heaven experienced here on earth

***Mercy:** Compassion shown especially to an offender or one subject to one's power

Mercy

More than an
Emotion, it's a
Readiness to
Cancel out what someone may owe
You, even when that person may not appear to deserve it

Moved in your
Emotions to
Release a debt and
Come to someone's aid, even though they may have treated
You unkindly and disrespectfully, you choose to help anyway.

Most High God's heart
Emotion
Released through us to
Care for one another
Yielding to be "Him" on the earth

Manifested
Empathy
Ready to
Care for someone or something, even if
You don't have personal connections other than hearing and answering "A Heart Cry."

Main thing
Everyone is in need of
Regardless of whether they know it or not, when it
Comes to needing a move of God's heart, especially when
You know you don't deserve it

***Hope:** To desire with expectation of fulfillment; One that gives promise for the future.

Hope

Help to
Overcome
Perceptions that
Evilly and erroneously say that nothing can ever change and get better

Heart
Opening
Position to
Encourage you while you wait for things you have applied your faith to, to come to pass

Hand up in
Overcoming
Pressure to
Entertain doubt

Herald (announces) the
Opposition to the
Pushback of
Every doubt that would say "there's no way"

Haven to house
Out-of-the-box
Problem-solving tactics that when
Engaged, bring about opportunity for change

Gifted: Talented

✝**Gifted:** Having exceptional talent or natural ability

Gifted

God's ability
In a particularly
Fashioned way
That makes it
Exceptionally easy to
Do or achieve something that may have been seen as unachievable

God granted
Insight given to individuals regarding
Future needs and solutions
That
Edify all those
Dependent on God for answers

Generous hearted
Individuals
Fashioned by God
To be an
Example of His
DNA (Divine Nature of the Almighty God)

Gracious
Individuals that
Find
That taking time with
Everyone who needs it
Demonstrates the Love of God

Genuinely
Invested individuals that
Find
Time to
Encourage those who
Don't see themselves as being worth investing in

***Help:** Aid, assist, relieve, promote, refrain from; prevent, remedy, relief; one who assists another

Hands-on
Effort to
Lend one's
Power to another for whatever is needed; assistive support

Only by the "grace" of God (His helping agent) can we survive for any length of time, despite the multitude of daily challenges that are becoming increasingly life-threatening.

***Meaningful:** Implication of a hidden significance; something helpful in achieving the desired end

***Bless (ed, ing)**: To invoke divine care for; to invoke divine favor upon; to ask God to look favorably on

Bless

Bestowing
Love on
Everyone who
Seems to need it,
Shoring up anyone for future success

Bringing
Love into
Evil
Situations to
Sever hurtful impact that would leave a residue of "scars"

Be a help in breaking the chains of
Lies that would
Evilly
Suggest that when trials come, it is because
Someone is being "cursed" by God

Bathing someone
Lavishly with
Everything that
Someone may need and want,
Sending a message to the heart that they are loved

Bravely
Loving when
Everything that has been
Said and done to you
Screams that you should do the "opposite."

Favor: When someone gives a blessing to another without a hidden agenda. This kind of favor is only possible because the heart of God's love has touched their heart to give it to you.

Favor

Father God's
Approval of our lives that
Visits (shows up) in the way of
Opportunities and our ability to
Recognize and take full advantage, knowing
He is with us to help make it "happen."

Found to be
An asset when
Venturing into
Often times
Relationships that need a bridge to connect people
together from all walks of life

Finds
A way to
Voice without words an
Opinion that suggests someone should be
Regarded with respect

Freedom from
Always feeling the need to be
Validated knowing that
Only God can
Really give validation that comes without strings

Friend inspiring connection that
Allows for
Various
Opportunities to be
Realized with a promise of help to inspire completion of any endeavor

***Gratitude:** Thankfulness; The quality of being thankful, readiness to show appreciation, and to return kindness

***Humility:** The quality or state of being humble.

Humility

Having the
Understanding that
Making the decision to
Invest in
Letting others shine or come first
In no way
Takes away from who
You are. On the contrary, when you don't insist on being in the spotlight, this speaks of the surety of knowing who you are.

Hope-filled
Undertaking regarding
Making the decision to
Ignore being considered
Less than, but
Instead, you then
Take being disrespected at times and
You concentrate on how you're "more than," because of how God sees you.

Houses
Unknown power
Making
It impossible to be
Led astray when you
Insist on
Taking time to be wise about what
You would or should not do when provoked.

Has the
Unlimited ability to
Make you an
Incredible
Leader
Illustrating what it
Takes for
You to be worthy to lead

Hidden power
Underneath
Many humiliating
Instances that
Led to your having to choose to
Invest in your
Trusting God to know what's best to get
You to the **Greatness** that awaits you from
your "**trust fund**."

Your awesome destiny
is being held in
***trust** for you.*

✣**Honor:** Adherence to what is right or standard of conduct

Honor: Appreciative reverence for or toward someone or something

Honor

Having feelings
Of appreciation for someone or something
Needing
Others to know about them
Regarding what you consider valuable

Having
Others observe you putting the
Needs of
Others before your own
Regarding not taking credit for team-related endeavors
and achievements

Having the fortitude to
Openly stand for right,
Not yielding to
Oppressive demands to do otherwise
Recognizing standing for right, even alone, is a worthy
reverent valuable thing to do

Hosting an
Open display of appreciation that
Now can be
Observed by others who can
Recognize and appreciatively join in

Holy (sacred)
Outpouring of expressions of appreciation
Needing to be let
Out to bring
Relief of release from grateful hearts to those who
deserve it

Respect: To recognize and show the worth of a person or thing; to treat with the intent of showing consideration for someone's value

Respect

Realization that
Everyone
Should be treated as if they matter,
Putting an
Ever-increasing well of
Caring
That others can take part in

Reviewed as one of the
Essentials of life to be
Shared and
Practiced by
Everyone
Causing a
Trickled down and up effect for all

Rescue tool when
Evil disrespect is afoot
Stopping the
Power of
Evil and
Creating a
Treatment of healing for those in need of it

Relenting to
Engage in the
Sacred
Practice of
Encouraging each other to
Care by
Treating each other with justifying kindness

Reserved
Expression for
Someone who has
Put you first
Even when they
Could have
Taken their time, energy, money, and care,
somewhere else or kept it for themselves

6/Six

Sign that
Insist anything can be
Xeroxed= Copied or repeated good or bad, if man
is in
the midst

Mankind: Everyone (man, woman, boy, girl); all races and creeds.

EVERYBODY!!!!

Multitude of multicultural,
Anything but ordinary,
No two are made exactly alike; one-of-a-
Kind
Individuals
Needing to know that they
Don't have to be accepted by any particular race or creed to be considered valuable in the sight of God

***People:** Human beings making up a group or linked by a common characteristic or interest; human beings; the mass of persons in a community or a body of persons (as a tribe, nation, or race) united by a common culture, sense of kinship, or political organization.

Human-Kind: For those sensitive to the word "mankind."

Hued, multi-colored
Underrated
Miraculous manifestations of
Almight God
Not always aware that all are

Kings and Queens that
Invites
Negative interaction from their not knowing bringing about
Divisive conflicts regarding "mistaken identities"

***Community:** a locality where people reside

Coming together
Of people, hopefully with
Mutual goals and
Mindsets,
Understanding that
Nothing
Is impossible
To achieve when
You come into agreement for the greater good of *everyone*

Family: Those who are connected by blood or love

Foundation for
All
Matters when it comes to
Influencing
Lives for a greater
Yield of success

We must treat the family as the most important treasure to be a good steward of.

I, Me, My, Mine, You, Them, They, Their, We, Us, Our, Your, Yours, He, She, Him, His, Her, Theirs, Myself, Herself, Himself, Yourself, etc.:

These pronouns can be the subject of your number messages when the number **6** is involved.

Example: You may have something heavy on your mind about your future. God allows you to see a set of numbers, "6559." You may hear what God says to you through these numbers: "***<u>You</u>*** *<u>have</u> Greater Still Grace for the future."*

You, in turn, can receive what He's saying and now affirm to yourself by making it personal. The numbers now become, "***<u>I</u>*** *<u>have</u> Greater Still Grace for the future*" from you embracing what He said.

All of me
All of you
All of him
All of her
All of us
All of them

These **sight** words you could hear in your conversation with God.

Specified or singled out as to which
Individual (s) or
Groups or things
Having
The "subject" placement in your personal conversation with God

Essential to help with journaling

7/Seven

Served as an

Eye-opening

Venture into believing that

Everything is purpose-filled.

Nothing is by chance.

***Absolutely:** Without exception, completely, wholly, entirely. Without a doubt or reservation, positively, certainly.

***Win:** To get possession of by effort to obtain by work

Weathering through (chipping away at mountainous situations) by
Investing in
Never allowing fear to keep you from pursuing your goals, one chip, one step at a time.

***Fulfill (ed, ing, ment):** To put into effect; to bring an end; to satisfy

***Complete (ly, ness, ion, ed, ing):** To make whole or perfect, having all parts or elements ended; fully carried out; finished; concluded

Done: As in "it's over," completely finished

***Perfect (ly, ing, ed, ion):** Being without fault or defect; exact; precise; to make perfect

Okay

Overall you can
Keep going in an
All is well, attitude while
You are achieving goals with an *"eye wink"* permission slip from God

***Eminent:** Used to emphasize the presence of a positive quality; standing above others, especially in rank, work, or achievement

Correct (ed, ing, ion, ive, ly, ness): To put right what may be wrong

***Whole (ly, ness):** Being in healthy or sound condition; free from defect or damage; not scattered or divided; nothing missing

Everything: All-inclusive

Content: Satisfied

Enough: Nothing else is needed; no lack

***Balance (d):** To arrange so that one set of elements equals another; to bring or come to a state or position of balance; to bring into harmony or proportion

***Total (ed, ly):** Making up a whole; entire amount; complete

Discipline: Training that corrects, molds, and perfects; control gained by obedience or training; orderly conduct; training or development by instruction and exercise (practice), especially in self-control.

***Stretch (ed, ing):** To become extended without breaking. An act of extending or drawing out beyond ordinary or normal limits.

***Endurance:** The ability to withstand hardship and stress; fortitude

Intentional (ly): The state of mind with which an act is done; purposeful; directed with keen attention; a determination to act in a certain way

***Predestine:** To settle beforehand; to foreordain

***Determined:** Firmly resolved; to settle, to fix conclusively or authoritatively, to come to a decision

Solid: Thoroughly dependable; reliable; serious in purpose and character

Sound:

1) Not diseased or sickly
2) Free from flaws or defects
3) Free from error or fallacy
4) Legal, valid
5) Firm and Strong
6) Thorough
7) Undisturbed
8) Showing good judgment

***Exactly:** Precisely, accurately, or correctly.

Forever and Always: No beginning; no end

***Sufficient**: Adequate to accomplish a purpose or meet a need

Truthful: The state of being accurately honest, omitting nothing

True: Without variation

Trustworthy: Reliable; dependable; faithful

Wholeheartedly: Undivided in purpose or will

Guaranty (eed): To give an agreement or an assurance that a particular thing will take place; an insured promise

✟**End:** A final part of something, especially a period of time, an activity, or a story; come or bring to a final point; finish; conclusion

Electing to
Not
Dally, procrastinate, abort, or surrender (give up) before the intended goal is achieved

Remnant

Remaining part of the
End that is
Meant to
Now
Anchor and reveal what was the
Nature of
The thing or situation, and what or who's left to tell the story.

***Positive (ly, ity):** Affirmative; confident, certain as inconclusive, as in favorable

Powerful, perfecting attitude that promises an
Overcoming
Spirit that
Insures
There
Is a
Victory is waiting when we
Endure To The End

Finish (ed, ing): Bring to a conclusion

***Protect (ed, ing, or, ion):** To shield from injury or harm

Preserve: Maintain wholeness; keep healthy; protect; keep alive; keep intact

***Converge (ed, ing, ance, nt):** To approach one common center or single point

Connect (ed, ing, ion): Linked together.

***Togetherness:** In or into harmony; coherence

Solution: Best plan to solve a problem

Change for the Better: Change that increases the ability for improvement, perfecting, and correcting growth, although it may have some hardship moments and seasons to bring forth the need and desire for change, regardless of what it looks like. God is in it with you.

Reaching out to close the gap

To Teach Truth: To teach the whole of something.

Teach and Reach: To educate whoever is open to learning.

Bridge a Gap

Be a
Reliable
Individual who
Demonstrates
God's love for
Everyone

And

Give others
A chance to
Practice doing the same without judging.

Practice (ed, ing, cal): To perform or work repeatedly to become proficient

Heal: Make whole

***Full:** Complete; satisfied; having volume or depth of sound; entirely; the highest or fullest state or degree; the utmost extent; the requisite or complete amount; maximum

Full Circle Moment

Finding out and
Understanding what
Led to
Long winding roads on your journey in life that were

Crucial
In your
Reveal of how
Capable you were in
Lasting through
Events and situations that

May not have made sense to your
Oppressed
Mindset until similar
Events and situations
Now show you
The truth about how all was needed to become the
now evolved **you**

Never Failing

Not
Even when
Violence and
Evil
Rage, shouting, "I'm in charge!"

Father God, in
All His power and glory,
Is here to
Lovingly but powerfully
Issue warrants for arrest from heaven that prove
No one is
Greater or more faithful in loving you by making---
All
Things
Work

"If and when you trust Him"

8/Eight

Entrance

Into

God

Having His way

To bring forth new life

Nu: New unlimited

New Birth: Delivered into new space

New Life: Never-before-seen creation

***Revive:** To bring back to life consciousness or activity; to make or become fresh or strong again

New Beginnings: Starting over

Procreate (tion): To be a part of a transfer from the heart of God into the earth, bringing forth "new life." * To bring forth offspring

New Beings: Newly created beings, different from those who came before

Nubee: Nickname for Nu "New Unlimited" being

***Rebirth:** Renaissance, revival

Resurgence of
Existence
Bring forth new
Identity
Revealing that a
Transformation
Has taken place

New Creation (s): Whatever has been created that doesn't have anything exactly like it

Recreate (d, ing, ion): To create again; refashion; reinvent

***Remake:** Make again; re-form; reshape; remodel; restyle; reproduce; reformat; change the format

***Redo:** To do over; recreate; repeat; restart; rebuild

***Reform:** To make better or improve by removal of faults; to form again

***Reproduce:** To produce again or anew

***Regenerate (ion):** To subject to spiritual renewal; to reform completely; to replace (a body part) by a new growth of tissue; to give new life to

***Refresh:** To revive by or as if by the renewal of supplies; to rejuvenate, to renovate, to refurbish

Made Over: Remake; remodel

Never Before Seen

Brand "NU" (New Unlimited) Start

Bold **R**adical **A**dvancement **N**ot **D**reading **N**egativity **U**nderstanding **S**ome **T**hings **A**re **R**escheduled **T**o give you time and wisdom to achieve all you desire to do.

Coming Attractions

Nu (New Unlimited) Experiences: New, unbelievable, unexpected happenings that can be yours

New Normal

Now is a never
Expected time
When

Nothing seems to be
Optional to
Realign in a
Manageable way that has to be
Acknowledged that it's time to
Learn a different way of thinking, doing, living, and being

No way the old way could
Ever be enough to help you
Win at

Navigating through or
Out of the
Regularly
Manageable ordeals when
All has changed, and
Leaning to refusing to accept it can and will cause painful hardship if not open to being teachable for a 'right-now' and future "win"

Just Getting Started

Juxtaposing (to permit comparison) of your
Understanding of what
Seems
To have

Gotten to the
End of a
Thing can now be
Thought of as the beginning
Initiative
Needed to
Get to the next level

Setting the
Tone and temper
Allowing for
Resets if needed while
Taking advantage of what's already been done to
Ensure the next step of expansion will be a
Detailed success

Begin Again

Be
Eager to
Give
It another try
Not

Always
Going back to what didn't work, but
Acknowledging
It's
Not what didn't happen, but what could work this time
with God's help

9/Nine

Next

In line to

Note that

Eternity exists on earth

***Power:** The ability to act or produce an effect; a position of ascendancy over others; authority; one who has control or authority; physical might; mental or moral vigor; force or energy used to do work.

Power: The act of magnifying, making bigger by bringing attention.

Life: An extension of heaven

Love in the form of the natural and spiritual essence of God's heart

Move (ment): To change or cause to change positions; to go from one point to another; to show marked activity; to take action; a calculated step to achieve an objective.

Life-Altering

Life-Producing

Life-Preserving

Life-Saving

***Fertile:** Producing plentifully; full of life

Fertilize: To unite within the process of fertilization; to come together to help things fruitfully grow; to produce life.

***Fruitful (ness, ly):** Very productive

Fruit Producer, Fruit Bearer: One who produces

Fruit Bearing, Fruit Producing: Supplying; to be the source of

Life: Dependency on God (nothing can live and/or grow healthily without Him)

***Healthy:** Enjoying or typical of good health; well; evincing (showing or revealing) or conducive to health; prosperous

***Flourish:** Prosper; to reach a height of development or influence

***Prosper (ing, ous, ity):** To succeed; to achieve success

Multiply (ied, ing): To increase exponentially.

***Success (ful, fully):** Favorable or desired outcome

Extravagant: Excessive; extreme amount

***Lavish:** Abundance; expending or bestowing profusely; to expend or give freely

***Vibrant:** Pulsating with life, vigor, or active sound from the vibration

***Fresh:** Received newly or anew; free from being tainted

Promise: A guarantee offered concerning something happening or being given in the future

***Possess (ion):** To have as property, own; to have as an attribute, knowledge, or skill; to enter into and control firmly

Destiny: A person's preordained future

Dreams: Wishes and wants; pictures of possible things to come

Today: The Increment of time that speaks of “now” is here

Time that is upon you to
Open God’s gift of life and
Determinately decide to get
All that
You can get out of it (enjoyment, an increase in goals achieved, love and happiness, etc.) that automatically paves the way to success

Future: Time that is to come

Tomorrow

Time when
Opportunity for a
Much better future can be seen as
Optional when
Reviewed through the eyes of hope to
Reveal unlimited
Options and possibilities
When you acknowledge and embrace where your help can come from.
Papa God’s grace is waiting.

***Foster (ed, ing):** Affording, receiving, or sharing nourishment or parental care though not related by blood or legal ties.

***Invest (ed, ing, ment):** To furnish with power or authority; to cover completely; clothe; adorn; to endow with a quality or characteristic; to make use of for future benefits or advantages; to involve or engage especially emotionally; to grant someone control or authority over, vest; to endow with a quality, infuse; envelop

***Supply:** To satisfy the needs; to provide

***Provision:** A measure taken beforehand to deal with a need or contingency

✝Fuel: To supply or power; to cause to burn more intensely

Super Abundant (ly): Extreme; more than enough; unlimited abundance

Nurture: To care for with the sole purpose of helping someone or something increase and mature.

***Prepare (ed, ing):** To make or get ready; to get ready beforehand

Process of
Readying,
Educating oneself or others to
Put into
Action all that is necessary to
Rightly
Execute what is needed to achieve a goal

***Thrive:** To grow luxuriously; to prosper

***Cultivate:** To foster growth; refine; improve; encourage

Rich (ly): Possessing or controlling great wealth; valuable; of great quality

***Satisfy:** Gratify; to make happy

Increase: Addition; expansion

***Measurable:** Able to be measured; something that can be quantified

Sowing and Reaping: For future fruitfulness

Sowing and **Reaping**

Seeding, giving in hopes
Of making a
Way for you and others to
Increase to fulfill
Needs to help people and things
Grow knowing that a

Return can be
Expected from
A
Promise of
Increase that has
Now been
Given by God (when sown with pure motives)

Sowing and **Reaping**

Simply put, it's a way to
Overcome a
Woe is Me, mindset, and
Invest in the
Next person
Giving them a hand up and over

Realizing that to do so is in
Everyone's best interests and benefits, where
All can
Prosper,
Inviting the
Next person to desire to
Give, creating a world of "caring."

Harvest Time

Having
Achieved after investing time, seed, and watering for
what you wanted, that you have now
Reached a point when you know
Virtually,
Everything that was
Sown has now
Turned into

The promise for
Increase and
More than
Enough for all to be embraced and enjoyed.

Due Season

Declared time
Under the watchful
Eyes of the Father, where

Something promised has
Entered into
A now timing,
Seen now as
Obtainable. All you
Need to do is recognize and embrace what time it is.

Do Season

Doing as
Opposed to

Selectively obeying to do what is said to be needed, but
Electing not to try reasoning it out, but
Always electing to follow through
Staying the course
On the promises of God
Not stopping because you can't see how the
"All Things Work"
Promise
Can and will work {Romans 8:28}

Demonstrate what it takes to
Overcome challenges by

Setting your
Eyes on the prize.
Address what may be
Slowing down your efforts to
Obtaining it and doing what's
Necessary, especially eliminating things that would waste time and energy that would keep you from reaching your goals.

✥**Follow:** To go or come after (a person or something proceeding ahead)

- Go after someone in order to observe or monitor
- Strive after; aim at
- Go along (a route or path)
- Keep track of, trace the movements or direction of
- Come after in time or order
- Happened after (something else) as a consequence
- Act according to (an instruction or precept)
- Conform to
- Act according to lead or example of (someone)
- Pay close attention to something

- Maintain awareness of the current state or progress of (events in a particular sphere or account)
- Be concerned with the development of something
- Undertake or carry out (a course of action or study)

***Follow:** To engage as a way of life

- Obey
- Pursue
- To come after in rank or natural sequence
- To keep one's attention fixed on

Form
Of
Leadership building,
Learning to be
Open to
Wisdom of those who have gone before you

***Forward:** Being near or at or belonging to the front

- Eager, ready
- Brash and bold
- Notably advanced or developed
- Moving, tending, or leading toward a position in front

- Extreme, radical
- Of relating to or getting ready for the future
- To or toward what is ahead or in front
- To help onward, advance

Frontier movement that
Opens up
Radical possibilities
Waiting for
Anyone
Ready and willing to
Daringly be different

Life Lesson (s): Living through instructional educating experiences found to be essential for living a life of excellence and success when submission to ongoing learning is seen as a necessity

***Fulfill (ed, ment):** To put in effect; to bring to an end; to satisfy

10/Ten

Time to tell the truth when

Enquiry is made

Negating lying doctrines disguised as foundations to believe and build on as well as pass on

***Supreme:** The ultimate highest rank or authority; highest in degree or quality

***Glorious:** Possessing or deserving glory; praiseworthy

Glory

God's
Luminous
Omnipotence
Released by a
Yes, that says you're welcome here

God’s
Love
Overwhelmingly
Released to help people
Yield to love

God's
Love-light that
Outshines anything or anyone with
Regards to who is superior in power and in caring that
You can yield to for your life

Foundational Doctrine: knowledge that can be the foundation to build on and increase

***Win:** To get possession of, to gain

Wisdom to
Insure that
Nothing can stop you from obtaining your goal

Statute (s): Written laws given by an authority to be used and followed for protection and corrective purposes

Set of stabilizing
Truths
Agreed upon
To be
Understood
That is what
Everyone will adhere to, to keep order

***Plan (ned, ing):** A method for accomplishing an objective or goal.

***Standard:** Something set up as a rule for measuring or as a model to be followed

Something of "substance"
To be
Acknowledged as
Needful when making a
Demarcation
As to what is a
Right way to
Do something to get a repeatable win

Boundaries: Something that marks or fixes a limit

Decree: An order made by a competent authority

Declaring of an
Edict: an official proclamation to be
Carried out
Regarding a coming
Event that would
Establish something or someone's placement in history

Testify: Tell it all --- Tell the truth --- with help from God.

***Sign:** An Omen (something that foreshadows a future event); a display to take notice of

Something used to
Instigate
Giving attention or
Notice to something meaningful. It also can be an omen, something that foreshadows a coming event.

Time: Increments of measurement of eternity on earth

Testifying
Informant that
Makes an
Ever-evolving case revealing that God is real

Symbol

Symbol: A thing that represents or stands for something else, especially a material object representing something abstract

Something
You used to
Make sense of things
Beyond mutual reference points in the imagination
department that allows
Others to be
Linked to some abstract reasoning brought to life

Wonder

Whatever may be seen to be
Out of the ordinary
Needing a
Definition that
Everyone can
Refer to
Also, it's a cause of astonishment or surprise, marvel,
miracle, or a feeling of awe.

Divine (Divinity): Relating to God being supremely good and heavenly

Detailed displays of
Irrefutable
Views and other stimulated senses that are
Impossible
Not to be attributed to an
Ethereal state of being--- heavenly in nature

Testimony

Telling of what has been
Experienced firsthand not
Something someone
Told you, but an
Illumination (to supply clear pictures) through
Making sure there are no
Omitting truths that could
Negate someone being able to
Yield to believing what you say is real

Keeping It Real

History: A chronological record of significant events, often with an explanation of their causes

Attest (ed, ing): To prove or declare to be true

Testify

Tell
Everything
Sharing
Truth that can
Illuminate that
Facts are only partial truths when
You're viewing a situation

Truth Be Told

The telling of what
Really took place
Understanding
That to
Halfway tell something, and then

Bother to
Embellish (add elements not true) is a crime against

Truth that
Only
Leads to the
Downfall, detriment to someone or something

✟**Test:** A procedure intended to establish the quality, performance, or reliability of something, especially before it is taken into widespread use; a short written or spoken examination of a person's proficiency or knowledge; an event or situation that reveals the strength or quality of someone or something, putting them under strain.

Test

The examining and proving of how well you have been
Equipped to
Sustain and survive
Trials and challenges in all areas of life

Glory Story

God's
Loving mercy that was present to help you
Overcome whatever test, trial, trouble, or trauma that tried to
Rule and run over
You that now you want to

Share
Telling everyone how you
Overcame, giving God thanks and
Referring others to
Yield and consider having an overcoming relationship with Him

The Glory Story is testifying of how you know it was God, His power, grace, and mercy that got you over and through whatever you know you couldn't have done without Him. It is the glorifying, the magnifying of who He was and is in the story. The announcement, declaration of gratitude to marvel in the truth, "He didn't have to do it, but He did." This was speaking of His love for you.

Divine Experiences

Denoted
Incredulous
Viewings of
Incredible, sometimes
Never before heard of or seen
Eye-popping

Encounters
E**X**citing and
Perplexing at the same time,
Each
Reaching beyond your earthly knowledge to have you
Inquire and
Enter into a time of
New
Chances to
Engage in the
Spirit realm with God

Great Grace

God's
Running over
Exponential (of an increase) and
Accelerated
Time and supply of

God-given
Resources
Accessed by
Calling out to Him, believing, and knowing His
Ears miss nothing (especially where we are concerned)
even when it doesn't seem like it

***Generous:** Free in giving or sharing; high-minded; noble; abundant; open-handed

***Examine (ed, ing, er):** To inspect closely; to test by questioning

***Total (ly):** To achieve the desired effect

***Recalling:** To call back; remember, recollect; revoke or cancel; a summons to return; rememberance of things learned or experienced

Spiritual Truth of Recalling

Recalling has the power to bring about repeats of anything good or bad when actions are applied.

Commandment (s): A direct order or instruction given by God is to be obeyed for righteousness and safety's sake; to be heard, received, embraced, observed, and acted upon to keep order and safety in an honorable way, agreeing that the Omniscient One (All-knowing) knows what's best.

Coming forth of
Orders and declarations to be followed
Making it easy for
Mankind to
Agree to
Network together and
Deciding to demonstrate what
Makes it possible for
Everyone to
Never be without the
Truth of how all can agree to get along in an honorable way

***Exorcise:** To get rid of by or as if by solemn command

11/Eleven

Everlasting testament of

Love

Engaging us in

Various ways, giving

Evidence that we are

Not alone (in anything)

***Justification:** Acceptable reason for doing something; the action of declaring or making right in the sight of God

Just the act of
Understanding that in
Some situations
Truth
Is more informative than
Facts that can be
Inconclusive and
Cannot give an
Accurate account regarding motives
That now can be
Interpreted as just and reasonable to have mercy applied to
Once found guilty verdicts changed to
Not guilty, and have it noted

5 + 6 = 11

Accepted mercy towards mankind = Justification

***Just:** Correct; proper; morally or legally right; deserved

Justice: Fairness; righteousness; righteous equality

***Justify (ied):** To prove to be just, right, or reasonable; to pronounce free from guilt or blame

When you give God your wrongs and ask Him to forgive in exchange, He **justifies** you.

Judges you with the
Understanding that you are
Saying you want Him to
Take whatever
It is, whatever is the
Fault and do the
Impossible by making it, in His
Eyes, as if it never happened,
Sealed with the promise that "*you're clean in My eyes*" is how He views you

Judgment: A decision made after reviewed facts are judged that can carry penalties of punishment regarding the right or wrong of a situation. Hopefully, God (the Omniscient One who knows everything) will be called upon in the decision-making because He is the only One who knows absolutely what was intentionally or ignorantly done. But no sentence has to be permanent if you are willing to ask for forgiveness.

Testimony of Unity: 10 Testimony of
+1 Unity
11

Glory Story of Oneness: 10 Glory Story
+1 Oneness
11

Trustworthy, Trust: Reliable, dependable, faithful

Forget: To be unable to think of or recall

***Forgive:** To give up resentment of

Forgive

Forego and
Opting out of
Replaying hurts and injuries
Given and done by
Individuals in
Various ways that may have been
Evilly intended, granting a release for you first and then them

Forgiven: The experience of knowing you have been pardoned and possibly released from punishment after being found guilty of wrongdoing

Forgiven

Feelings
Of gratefulness after being pardoned and
Released from
Guilt and shame for being
Involved in
Various things that
Ended
Negatively for someone else, where you were at fault

Forgiveness

Finding a way to be
Open to not demanding your
Right to have someone forever on the hook regarding
their having wronged you and being willing to
Give up
Insisting they be punished and
Volunteering to
Exercise mercy even though it's
Not
Easy and
Sometimes, don't make
Sense that you would do it

It is an "Unlimited Delivering Power"

***Exonerate:** Unburden; to free from blame

***Vindicate:** To avenge; to provide defense for; to maintain a right to

***Insure:** To make certain

Favor

Fear releasing
Agent that can
Vindicate us from
Oppressive evil
Reports that scream, *"No, you can't have it!!!"*

***Absolve, Absolution:** To set free from an obligation or the consequences of guilt

***Advocacy:** The act of advocating

***Advocate:** To plead in favor of: A person who publicly supports or recommends a particular policy.

Help: To come alongside to assist, to lend power to what could possibly not be done alone.

***Inspire:** To influence, move, or guide by divine or supernatural inspiration; to affect; to bring out or about

***Satisfy:** To answer or discharge (a claim) in full; to meet the requirements of; reparations for an insult and settlement for a claim; to make happy; to make complete

Standing in
Accountability so
Truth
In the
Situation can bring
Freedom to
You

Absolutely: Done deal; no takebacks

***Erase:** To rub or scratch out as written words

Erase

Eradicate,
Rub out until
All
Signs of a thing or situation are as if it had never
Existed

Cover: To protect; to shield; to hide; to conceal

Keep, Kept: To guard, to take care of, to maintain

Cover And Keep
Instructional
Covered And Kept
Declared Promise

Guarantee (d, ing): To give security to

✞**Bankable:** Certain to bring profit and success

Beyond
Any
Need of any
Kind, He is
Able and willing to
Bring or
Lead you to
Everything that would help you accomplish your goal if and when you trust Him. He is a "sure" thing.

***Especially:** Special, particularly

Qualified: Fit for a given purpose or job

Legitimate (ly): Genuine; sincere; real; authentic

Balance: Steadiness; stability; evened out

Equity: Having value in

Clearing: To remove

Validate: To demonstrate or support truth; prove the accuracy of something; approve of

***Confirm:** To give approval; to rectify; to make firm or firmer; to verify; to corroborate; to give proof

Vindicate: To clear of blame

Equality: Justness; evenhandedness; impartiality; fairness

Commit (ed, ment): To put into charge or trust; to carry into action; to pledge or assign to some particular course or use

Compassion (ate): Sympathetic feeling, pity

Mercy: Unearned forgiveness; clemency; having compassion for

Mercy

Mindful, heartfelt, God-given gift to be
Embraced and
Released
Concerning caring for and being intentionally kind, where
You have every right not to want to do it because of someone's words or actions that have put them in a place not to have earned such gracious treatment

Precious

Purposely considering and placing value when
Regarding
Everyone and anything that needs
Caring for
Irregardless
Of them not
Understanding their
Significance

Unconditional

Unbelievable at times,
Nurturing
Concept
Of
Never
Demanding that
Individuals do everything “right” before
They can be considered
In any way worthy
Of
Needing and getting an
Affirmation of
Love

Grace Sufficient

God's promise
Regarding
Anything that seems like you
Can't bear it,
Especially when it appears to be

Something that won't oppressively let
Up, attempting to
Force you into giving in to
Fear, forsaking knowing God is with you,
In spite of how "impossible" it
Continues to look.
It is not the truth. God is there. Truth is, He's
Enlarging and empowering you for the
Next good great
Thing He has planned for your life.

12/Twelve

The Most High God's

Way that lets

Everyone know who is to be the

Leader to lead

Various

Endeavors here on earth

Author (ed): One who brings into existence or creates

Always and forever, God's
Undisputable (unable to be challenged or denied)
True
Headship that's
Openly
Revealed

***Authority:** Power to influence thought or behavior; person in command

Acceptance of Responsibility

Author of Authority

Almighty sovereign creator God
Uses His
Throne room to
Hand down
Ordered
Responsibilities to those chosen to

Oversee and
Foster faith that hopefully

All would
Understand
That to
Have the
Opportunity to
Rule righteously
In any capacity
That it is not optional not to
Yield to the truth of where "true authority" comes
from

***Authorize (ed) Authorization:** To sanction; to give legal power to

Author of Time

Always and forever God who
Understands
That the vast infinitive nature of
Heaven would need to be
Offered to mankind in an "incremental way,"
Regulating an

Overwhelming need to be able to count or measure the existence into the
Future,

Taking
Into consideration how
Mankind, when only identifying with their human parts, is hard-pressed to
Embrace the very idea of "eternity."

In God's Timing

1	and	2	=	12
Uniquely		Set Apart		For such a time as this

The term ***"for such a time as this"*** refers to a specific time that has been uniquely kept secure and set apart to be revealed now.

Schedule

Setting a particular time for something to take place
Committing to keeping the appointment due to
Having prior knowledge of what's needed to
Eventually get something
Done,
Understanding that to
Leave it to chance is to invite
Everything and everyone to distract from starting and finishing your goals

***Authentic:** Genuine; real

***Origin (al):** Ancestry; beginning; the source

Lead (er)

Let
Everyone see you as an example by
Actually
Doing something first

Let
Everyone see you as an example by
Actually
Doing something first
Even though it may be
Regarded as being difficult or unpopular

Endow (ed): To furnish as with some talent, faculty, or quality; equip to provide for continuing support

Power

Putting forth the time and energy to
Overcome
Whatever is
Encroaching or attempting to "enforce" or
Rule over anything you have authority over

Position of ability to
Oversee and make decisions, and have them executed
Whether righteously or wickedly
Enforcing and
Regulating

Unity that secures, orders, and directs

12

1 and 2	1 and 2	1 and 2 .
Unity that secures	Unity that sets things in order	Unity that gives direction in an issue

***Order (ed, ing, ly, liness):** A specific rule, regulation, or authoritative direction; an arrangement; a specific sequence

***Destined:** To settle in advance; to designate, assign, or dedicate in advance; to direct or set apart for a specific purpose or place.

***Destiny:** Something to which a person or thing has been destined; a predetermined course of events.

***Providence:** Divine guidance or care; the quality or state of being provident (making provision for the future).

That's who God is

Ordained

Ordered steps
Revealed of
Demonstrating how
Almighty God has authorized and
Implemented what in life has your
Name on it that has now come forth from
Eternity to be
Declared and acknowledged here on earth

***Guarantee (ed, ing, or):** To give security to

***Conduct (ed, ing, or):** To direct; to act as a medium of conveying or transmitting

Statute: A law enacted by a legislative body; written laws given by an authority to be used and followed for protection and corrective purposes

***Sanction (ed, ing):** To give approval of; to endorse; to accredit

"I Got the Go-Ahead."

***Call (ed, ing):** To announce authoritatively; to summon; to make a request or command to come forth; to a position to be filled

***Outfit (ted):** The equipment or apparel for a special purpose or occasion; equip (ped)

"Loaded with what it takes"

Grants Permission: To bestow; a granting of consent in the use of authority

Guaranteed Strategy: A sure plan or method for achieving an end

***Command:** To direct authoritatively; order, govern, to overlook (see) from a strategic position; ability to control

***Organize (ed):** To form into a complete and functioning whole; to set up an administrative structure; to arrange by systematic planning and united effort

***Establish:** To set up; to gain recognition; to prove

License Provided: Released to use the authority given by a higher authority

Professional: One who has perfected a skill or talent with practice and continuous awareness of keeping abreast of new ways to do what they are called to.

Predominate: To be superior in power or numbers; prevail

Preeminent: Having the highest rank; outstanding.

Glory Story of Being Set Apart: 10 Glory Story of being
+2 Set Apart
12

"A Right to Stand In"

"A Right to Stand Up"

13/Thirteen

The

Hidden things of God being

Illuminated, brought to life

Regarding the

Truth of whether or not

Everyone who is

Exposed to the truth will decide whether or not they

Need to move from the dark, restrictive places, where **lies** limit us or into the expansive unlimited light of God's Greater, which is granted through truth. Truth will set and make you “free.”

***Deliver (ed, ing, er):** To set free; to give birth to; to utter; to communicate; to convey; to transfer

Deliverance is, after a struggle to be free, the process of bringing something to an end that is unacceptable to live free and thrive, doing whatever it takes to help bring that into manifestation, because that is our God-given right.

Deliberately choosing to
Exit out of small restrictive situations to enter into
Levels of more than enough to leave behind
Insufficient "spaces" for "greater," which sometimes are
Violently opposed by
Entities that have laid claim to your
Right to be free and won't
Accept
Not being able to keep you
Chained to
Everything and everyone that keeps you living in
restricted spaces:
Abusive relationships
Illnesses
Addictions
Religious factions
Political factions

Uniquely God Sculpted

1 and 3

Unique Miracles

Unique Miracle (s): Tailor-made for the need

Freedom: To be set free

***Release:** An act of setting free

Unifying Power: 1 and 3
Unifying Power

Deliberate: To consider carefully; determine after careful thought; done or said intentionally.

⌖**Resigned:** Having accepted something unpleasant that one cannot do anything about.

With God, resigned means

Resolute about
Entering into a
Settled state to watch what you've
Invested in,
Gain momentum and
Not negate the
Effort made by
Doubting the outcome that's been promised, making decisions to move, upsetting what's been set because of delayed manifestation of intended goals

Ready to
Embrace
Switching
Into a
Gear that will bring about the
Next step of progress
Even though it appears to be a
Defeatist move

Intentional: The state of mind with which an act is done purposefully; directed with keen attention; a determination to act in a certain way

Rebellion: The warring and struggle to be released from what appears to someone as unacceptable confinement against their will

Regarded most times to be
Evil when no one
Bothers to
Enquire what
Led to the need for
Liberation from
Intentional or ignorant
Oppressive situations
Negatively impacting a life

Rejecting righteous living practices and
Encouraging others to do the same
By
Evilly
Lying about what's being
Lost
If
Observance of rules are obeyed that are
Needed to ensure safety for all

Escape: Flight to get away; an exodus; running away.

Liberty: Authorized permission; independence; freedom

Arranged (ment): Decided agreement; to put in order

14/Fourteen

First to

Oppose evil.

Understand the misunderstood.

Right wrongs.

Take charge when no one else wants to lead.

Endure when all others won't and

Enlist other 1st responders willing to

Network so everyone can be saved.

10 + 4 = 14

Glory Story
of
Creation

Salvation: The saving of a person; the saving from danger, difficulty, or evil; the saving of a person from sin or its consequences in life after death

Saved (ing), Safe, Safety, Safely: Free from harm or risk; secure from danger or loss; to preserve

Savior: One who saves

***Rescue:** To free from danger, harm, or confinement

Retrieval from
Evil
Situations that
Can
Undermine anyone
Ever being free

***Salvage (ed, ing, able):** Things saved from loss or destruction; to rescue from destruction

14 = 1 and 4
Saving through unique interventions

***Help:** Aid, assist, improve, relieve; to be of use, promote; to refrain from, prevent; a source of aid; remedy, relief, one who assists another

Hands over
Ego to show
Love and
Prosper someone just because they need it

Has an
Effect of
Leaving a
Person in a better place than where they started.

Having someone or something provide
Effort to
Lessen the strain of some
Problem or situation

I

Got

You !!!

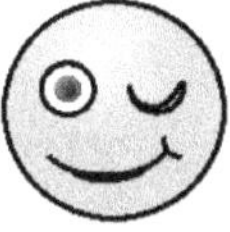

All Things Work: 1 and 4 = 14

All Things Work Salvation

Principle of

Anything that appears to
Leave a mark of
Lingering doubt

That
Has an
Impact that infers
Negatively that
God couldn't have possibly
Seen this coming, or He

Would have done something to block the
Outrageously oppressive thing, not
Realizing He is equipping you with all
Kinds of ways to be the overcomer that you have yet to meet

Prosper (ity, ous); Succeed: Thriving condition; success; to succeed in an enterprise or activity; to achieve economic success; to become strong and flourishing in health and wealth

Dependence: The state of needing something or someone for support or help. It is your need to rely on something or someone to succeed or survive.

Protect (ion): To grant safety; to keep safe; to cover; to defend

***Insurance:** A means of guaranteeing protection or safety

***Heal (ed, ing, er):** To make or become healthy, **sound**, or whole; to cure

Sound:

1) Not diseased or sickly
2) Free from flaws or defects
3) Free from error or fallacy
4) Legal, valid
5) Firm and strong
6) Thorough
7) Undisturbed
8) Showing good judgment

***Freedom:** The quality or state of being free or independent; release

Free: A state of mind in which one knows that they can choose to be and do without hindrance

Liberty: Authorized permission; independence

Loosed from
Inhibiting ideas or
Brainwashing that
Encouraged you to allow anyone or anything to
Rule over you
To take away your ability to know
You have the authority always to decide for yourself the best 'yes' or 'no' answer to fit any given situation

Safe and Sound

State of being
Acknowledged
For someone to be at
Ease when there has been

Any previous
Notification of dysfunction or threat of
Danger that

Since announced, has been
Opposed and defeated or corrected, leaving an
Understood knowledge, there is
Now nothing to be
Disturbed or frightened by

***Wholeness:** Being in healthy or sound condition; free from defect or damage; not scattered or divided; nothing missing

Well-Being: Sense of "All is well"

Enough: Nothing else is needed

***Wealth:** Prosperity; affluence; material riches; excessive means and capital; abundance of possessions

Where
Everyone
Actually
Learns
That living in
Harmony with each other is priceless

What is
Evident
After
Love
Teaches you
How to judge what is important

Worry-free, knowing that
Everything in God's
*"**A**ll Things Work"* promise
Lends to our
Trusting that
He is with us in every situation to make up the difference when we can't

When your
Essential needs
Are met, and you acknowledge that others who have
Less
That they can depend on, they would count themselves rich if they
Had what you have

Wealth of Health

Wisdom to
Engage and challenge
All adversaries coming against your
Life while
Trusting God to
Heal you

Of
Fear while

Helping you to be at
Ease but
Alert through the
Life lessons
That can be learned while
Healing is taking place

Glory Story of Creation

God's
Loving
Oration
Regaling how
You and I came to be

Sharing
The truth of how the
Omnipotent, Omniscient, Omnipresent, Most High God
Regarded having His "royal lineage" in
You and me,

Officiate over the state of affairs here on earth.
For the purposes of the fruitfulness of "free-will" beings,
moving Him to

Continue the
Royal lineage in the
Earth so
All would have a chance to reign
Together
Including all
On one accord with
Nature.

Uni (s) Create (ed, ing, ors, tion): <u>1 and 4</u>
Uni Create

Uni is a nickname for everyone, for we are all "unique" creations, and like God, we have the ability to create.

✞**Self-Sacrificing:** Giving up one's interest or wishes to help others or advance a cause together

Secure: Safe; protected; self-confident; fixed firmly

Breakthrough

Bright light of truth to help
Reach the other side of
Extremely tough times that
Appears to be the
Kind
That would never yield, and almost
Had you
Ready to give up before finally
Overcoming the lack of
Understanding that
God
Had your victory waiting for you while building faith and endurance

15/Fifteen

Rest & Restoration

Final outcome when anyone is willing to

Invest in believing that God knows what the

Future holds, as He is the One who holds

The future

Even when it seems as if

Everything going on would indicate or imply that He is

Not even paying attention, or if He sees whether or not He even cares.

We can "rest" in knowing He does see and He does care.

Rest

***Rest:** Sleep; freedom from work or activity; motionlessness or inactivity; a place of shelter or lodging; something used as a support; to remain based or founded; to cause to be firmly fixed; ground; dependant

Relinquishing control of
Everything while
Simply
Trusting everything will be alright

Realigning your very
Existence by releasing
Stress about things
That you cannot change

Relax and
Enter into a
State of
True peace

Remembering
Even if you
Stayed awake,
That doesn't ensure that anything you didn't want to happen, won't happen

Regain
Energy by
Staying still for a
Time

Reactivating agent that
Ensures us
Some down
Time to prepare for future productivity

Requirement for you
Ever
Solidifying your
Trust in God

Really make an
Effort to
Stay still
To regroup

Rapid-fire way to
Engage in
Something
That's replenishing

Release
Everything and everyone
So you can
Take a proper break

Room made to
Encourage
Sleep to
Take you out of work mode

Relief from
Everything
Stressful for a serious
Time out

Reset time to be
Enjoyed by
Simply refusing
To reject it

Removal from
Energy-draining
Situations
That would leave you
high and dry

Reality check
Everything and everyone must
Stay still for a
Time of renewal. Even batteries must be
recharged.

***Wait (ing):** To remain inactive in readiness or expectation; rest assured

Rest-filled: Peace of mind

✞Restful: Having a quiet and soothing quality

***Retire:** To withdraw, especially for privacy; to withdraw from one's occupation or position; to conclude one's career; to go to bed

***Repair:** To restore to good condition, fix; to restore to a healthy state

Backtrack

Being
Able to
Come to grips with
Knowing
That the only
Real way to go forward is to
Acknowledge what hadn't been
Considered can now, with new
Knowledge help achieve your goals

Sometimes going back to the last place of assured success can help you move forward.

***Restore (ed, ing, er):** To give back; return; to put or bring back into a formal or original state

Restoration

When there appears to be no one to hold responsible for what is lost, missing, or stolen, God wants us to know that He will restore it if we stop working and stressing about finding someone to blame. Just ask Him to give it back.

Return of
Everything that in
Some way was lost
Taken or conned
Out of you in
Regards to
Actions by you or others
That left you in a deficit,
Is now being replaced. You
Only
Need to ask and be willing to inquire about wisdom to keep what's being restored by doing it God's way.

***Revitalize (d):** To give new life or vigor to

Turn Around: Situations being turned in your favor.

Comeback: Can be achieved with an overcoming mentality that speaks to any perceived loss or defeat. "I will be back and come to win this time!"

Courageous
Overcoming
Mentality that manifests into
Endurance
Being made into
An action that
Can
Kick-Start a miraculous achievement of any kind

Restitution: The act of restoring; the state of being restored; restoring something to its rightful owner; making amends after causing loss or injury to someone.

***Revive (ed, ing):** To bring back to life; make or become fresh or strong again

Remember: To put back together what has been dismembered (that which has been torn apart, cut off, or separated from the whole) * Commemorate (to recall or bring to mind); to keep from forgetting; to recollect

Reproduce (tion) with God	**is an**	**<u>1</u>** **Uniquely**	**<u>and</u>**	**<u>5</u>** **Graced (ability)**	**<u>=</u>** **to**	**<u>15</u>** **Reproduce**

***Replace:** To restore to a former place or position; to take the place of; supplant (take the place of another, especially by force or trickery); to put something new in the place of

***Return:** To put back to or in a formal place or state; the act of returning something

***Find:** To meet with, either by chance or by searching or study; encounter. Discover; to obtain by effort or management; to arrive at; experience, feel; to gain or regain the use of; to determine and make a statement about; a valuable item of discovery

***Rescue (ed, ing):** To free from danger, harm, or confinement

Unifying Grace: <u>1 and 5</u>
Unifying Grace

United By Grace: <u>1 and 5</u>
United by Grace

United Gracefully: <u>1 and 5</u>
United Gracefully

Repent (ance): To change your mind, actions, and directions; deciding to go in the way of what God says is good and acceptable

Repent

Recognizing
Erroneous and evil ways
Practiced and deciding to
Evoke
Notice of eviction for
Trespass

Repentance

Resolute in respecting
Eviction
Process of
Erroneous and evil lifestyles (thoughts and deeds) by
Now
Taking time to
Acknowledge your part so you
Now
Can
Evict and close doors and openings to bar entrance for those things to return in the future with God's help

***Recompense:** To give compensation to; to repay, reimburse

Relax, Relaxation: Let go; to be at ease, to rest.

***Refresh (ing, ed, ment):** To make or become fresh or fresher; to revive by or as if renewal by supplies

Recreation: Actions that enhance enjoyment in life that allow for the increase of your being; "refreshed" for future endeavors; *a refreshing of strength or spirit after work; fun amusement

Fun: Pleasurable; entertaining, merriment, amusement

FUN

Found in
Understanding it's
Not natural to work without implementing some rest,
relaxation and
recreational things
in life

Peace: An inner harmony with self, tranquility, serenity

16/Sixteen

Simply stated,

It is the number sign for Love (16: 1=unity and 6=mankind) that needs to be

Xeroxed, repeatedly copied to

Tell and show

Everybody what can be achieved when we

Each decide to

Need one another (For Love's sake)

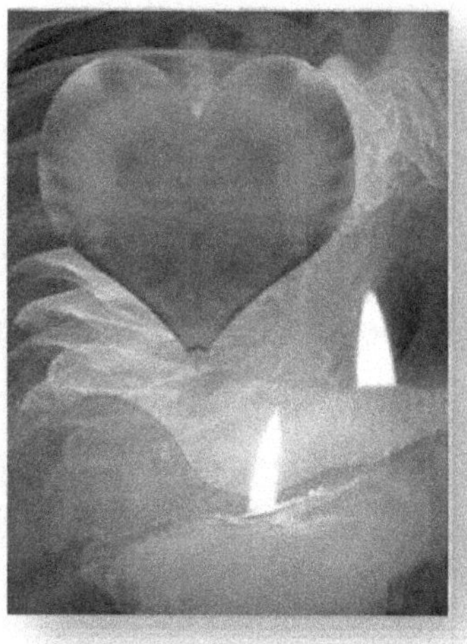

God Is Love

Leader from heaven
Overseeing every heart that
Volunteers to be open for
Entrance for Him to come in and reside (live with you)

Leveling powerful
Overcoming
Victorious
Equalizer

Lavish, extravagant gift given to
Others so that they can experience the
Very real
Existence of heaven here on earth

God Who Is Love

The Loving Lover of Our Souls
Who is Lovely to Behold

Glory Story of Man: God's Glorious Interaction with mankind

	10	Glory Story of
	+6	Man
	16	Love

All of Us **<u>1 and 6 = 16 in unity with each other</u>**
All of Us together = LOVE

***Together (ness):** In or into harmony or coherence

Romance (ed, ing): A romantic attachment; having an imaginative or emotional appeal

Intimacy: Of a very personal or private nature

Investment in a
Nature of
Trust that
Involves
Making room and giving
Access to the inner
Cores of
Your being

Respect: You accept someone for who they are, even when they're different from you, to honor

Real
Earnest way to
Sure up someone
Putting them at
Ease to be willing to
Come
Together for whatever is needed or wanted to be achieved (Relationships of all kinds)

Relationship building and an
Encouragement for
Someone to see
People with
Eyes of
Caring and a willingness
To treat them right

Share (ed, ing): To use and enjoy with others

***Gift:** Something given; the act or power of giving

Heart: The instrument used for pumping life-sustaining blood throughout the body; ✝the central or innermost part of something * the emotional or moral distinguished from the intellectual nature

Headquarters of
Everyone when
Acknowledging
Right or wrong,
The "truth" of it

Care: Watchful or protective attention; to feel concern or interest (God's eyes are always upon us, especially individually, to help when needed).

***Pleasure:** Desire; state of gratification; enjoyment; a source of delight or joy

Enjoyment: Delight; experiencing satisfaction; fun

17/Seventeen

Speaks of
Everyone being
Victorious when we
Esteem one another and measure success by
how well we meet each other's
Needs,
Taking
Every opportunity to
Engage in encouraging the
Next person unaware at times of how this, alone,
can change THE WORLD

***Win:** To be the victor

1 and 7
Unity Perfected

Willingness to
Invest in
Networking

***Score:** Reason, ground; success in obtaining something; to gain or tally as if in a game; record

Record

Rehearse **e**vents **c**onsidered to be **o**vercoming, **r**efusing to dwell on **d**efeats

Victory, Victorious, Victoriously, Victor

Victory

Very
Intentional
Concentrated effort
That
Overcomes just because you
Refuse to
Yield to Fear

***Triumphant:** Notably successful

Tested and tried to
Reveal how
Incredible and
Uniquely you are
Made that
Proves
How you
Always had what was
Needed
To be and do whatever

1	**AND**	**7**	**=**	**17**
Unique		**Endurance**		**The Win**

Overcome (er, ing): Overcome; to conquer

Outstanding point of
View
Encourages everyone to
Regard and treat
Challenge as an
Opportunity to
Make an
Example of what it looks like to win by doing it
afraid if necessary.

Succeed (ed, ing): To obtain a desired objective or end.

***Success (ful, fully):** Favorable or desired outcome

Uniquely Perfecting: One-of-a-kind, tailor-making; forming, molding; equipping someone for who they are to be and what they have been created for

*__A Master Piece:__ Work done with extraordinary skill.

Master Piece

Made to be **a** **s**pecial **t**ype of **e**ye-catching, wonderous **r**eveal, a **p**ortrait so distinct and **i**ndividualized that only trained **e**yes **c**an see what is **e**vident in the eyes of God.

That's who we are. 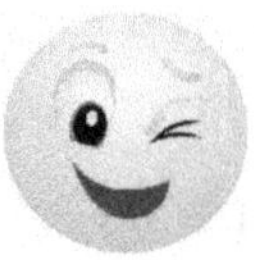

Unity Perfected: 1 and 7

Unity Perfected

Understanding that
Neglect of
Inclusion will continue
To tear us apart if we don't decide to
Yield to

Putting
Each other first by
Regarding rights and
Feelings
Eventually
Causing a "chain reaction" in how we
Treat
Each other that
Demonstrates "oneness" with all mankind

17

RICH

Recognizing what's
Important, investing in
Care for a
Harvest to be a blessing where there's a need
with whatever care (support) is needed
with whatever you have

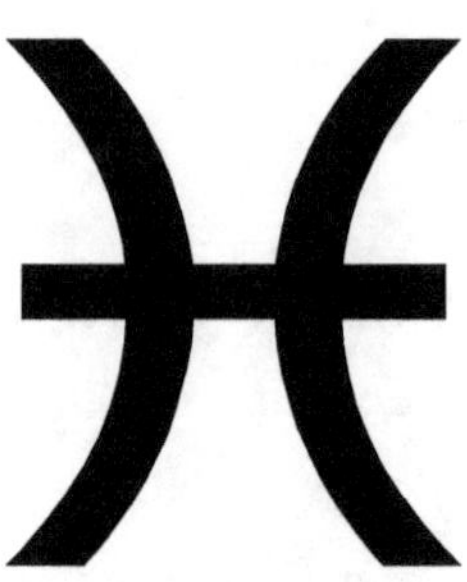

The scripture Psalm 91:16 says, "With long life, you, God, <u>will satisfy me</u> and show me your salvation."

18/Eighteen

Ever evolving

Illumination of

God's

Hidden plans for good

That

Everyone can

Eagerly look for, even though

Not without sometimes being challenged to the "hilt" to release the former (the old) in order to bring forth "The Nu" (new unlimited)

Testimony of Nu: 10 + 8

Testimony of New Unlimited

Telling of
Every
Story
That substantiates (proves) what once seemed
Impossible is now
Made possible by the
Omnipotent maker of all things
New, regarding
You and I being able to

Observe and possess all the good and great things
For our future of

New
Unlimitedness

Glorious Nu Beginnings: 10 + 8

Glorious Nu Beginnings

God's
Lavishly, loving
Overcoming Spirit
Rescuing and making the
Impossible things possible to
Overcome and
Understand He has
So much more in store from

New
Unlimited flows of grace, mercy, provision, etc.

Being brought forth into the
Earth for us to
Gather and give,
Insisting that all would
Now experience God's love that absolutely
No one would be excluded, but
Invited to be included in the
New unlimited flows of
God in everything. He is willing and waiting to
Share with us just for the asking.

End of Bondage

Every
Negative thing that has
Doggedly dragged

On and on and on
For what seems like forever is now

Being brought to a stop, put
On
Notice, issued that they
Don't have any more time left to stay. Then
Asking
God to help you
Execute evictions on everything evil whose expiration
date is your choice to demand it to be "now."

Delivering Grace: 13 + 5 = 18

Delivering Grace — Breaking of Bondages

Leading to ---- 18
Glorious Nu Beginnings

Demonstration of
Exercising the
License to
Insist in
Various ways that
Everything or everyone who
Refuses to meet your rights as
Important, must
Now be
Given "the boot" and by the

God-given
Righteous
Authority of "free will" you
Can
Execute the orders 'for them to go' or 'for you to leave,' whichever suits you

Breaking of Bondages

Boldly
Requiring
Examination of self
Acknowledging what
Kind of character or lack thereof
Is causing
Negative situations that with
God's help can be

Overcome
For a future

Bright with
Options … possibilities
Never before
Dreamed of
Allowing for
Great
Expectations to be realized and
Satisfied

Brainwashings
Rectified with
Education that edifies and eradicates (uproots)
All
Knowledge
Infested … laced with lies about
Not needing
God to help you

Overcome whatever is keeping you
From

Being able to
Oppose and overcome
Negative, evil elements
Dragging you
Against your will in and out of things when, with
God's help is not an
Even fight due to God being All-Powerful to
set you free. Just come into agreement and
"Watch"
Him
Work!!!

Being
Ready to
Eliminate
All that has been
Keeping you bound to a 'lesser-than-state' by
Insisting that there's
No way
God cares about what you're going through, but you decide to find

Out
For yourself by

Being
Open to let God know you
Need Him to come
Down into your life
And
Give permission for Him to
Elucidate (make clear) and realize everything that
Seeks to keep you from the best God has for you

Bold
Radical
Emissions of
Acknowledging you
Know that
In
Negative situations and hard times
God is able to deliver you

Out of them all …
From those known and unknown

Both now and in the future an
Overcoming plan of escape and victory in every situation
Notwithstanding the timing that sometimes appears
Delayed that
All-things-work is
God's promise for
Everyone looking to you to be
Set free

Unity Renewed: Where there once was 'unity' that has been fractured is now being renewed.

1 and 8
Unity Renewed

Undergirding support for the
Next
Individual who needs it
That will start a
Yielding to be kind. A sign that will bring

Reviving restoration of our original
Existence when everyone and everything in
Nature
Existed
With one aim: to live life in the
Earth the way it is in heaven, and
Demonstrate what that looks like.

Glorious Nu Being

God enlightened
Life
Of
Realizing there
Is
Only one greater than you
Understanding He (God) is the
Substance of your existence that leaves

No need to ever feel the necessity to attempt to
Usurp His authority

Because of the
Evidence of your being made
In His image and likeness, which
Now
Gives way to an agreement to accept and embrace you
and God being One

GLORIOUSLY JUST GETTING STARTED

19/Nineteen

Nexus (connection link)
In investigating and investing in what's
Needed to
Engage, endure, and go
Through this life
Encouraged and
Energized enough to make it to the
Next level, having faith that eventually,
everything will be alright

FAITH

Faintest to the most fierce
Agreement to
Invest your
Trust in what or whom you
Have been taught to believe in

FYI.

Everyone has faith in something or someone. It's impossible not to have faith because God gave us all the ability and a measure of faith to do with as our free will allows.

So, even if you believe that

"You have no faith,"

that only means you just placed

your faith in a

lie.

Honored Steps of Faith

Steps to a **sure-footed, deep-rooted faith** start with one step at a time. Allow God to help you up the steps.

1. **I can't!** (for whatever reason) He's not angry or afraid of your "I can't." He knows how you got there.
2. **Can I?** Is it really possible or sensible?
3. **Hope**--- I wanna believe.
4. **Believe**--- Trusting in whatever knowledge seems trustworthy, but remember, beliefs can be replaced.
5. **I Know**--- That which you know to be true because you lived it!!!

("**I Know**" is the "Gold" standard)

Papa God wants you to know He honors your steps of faith in Him until you can fully release yourself into trusting Him.

I encourage you to start stepping out in your faith walk with Him. He will be there to help you with whatever step you find yourself on and help lift you up until you reach the last step--- "**I Know**."

Forerunner to
Achieving the once thought to be
Impossible,
Trusting that anything is achievable with God's
Help

First
And foremost
Is indeed
Transferrable from
Heaven to here and from here to heaven.

Fast
Acting agent for
Increasing
The
Hope factor to believing

Former
Ancient of Days
Insert given
To
Help us with whatever (?)

Fence that grants
Ability to fend off
Intruding
Thoughts of doubt and
Hold on to dreams and promises

Flat out
Acknowledgment that
Indeed
There is nothing you can't
Have with determination and God's blessing

Fear-fighting
Agent that can come against any
Invading
Thoughts that would
Hinder your belief in what's possible

Forging
Ahead by
Including
The
Help from heaven to help you hold on to "hope"

Frequent
Acknowledgment of the
Irrefutable perfect
Timing of God to
Help you wait for the dream, vision, or promise to come to pass

Forever
Assistance when
It comes
To
Having the right mindset to achieve your goals

Fire that can
Actually
Ignite
Trust to
Hasten the promise to any manifested state

Fierce
Assault weapon that can
Incinerate “burn up or down”
Thoughts that
Have you doubting the possibility of success

Flare that can
Actually
Illuminate
The way to the
Help you need to hold on

Friend who keeps you from
Aborting (killing your dreams) by
Insisting
That you stay focused and
Hopeful

Force to be reckoned with when
Advancing
In the
Trust arena while
Having to wait on whatever

Flashlight to
Accurately
Illuminate the
Truth that may have been
Hidden in the darkness of doubt

Freedom from
Agonizing
Interrupting
Thoughts of doubt that
Hinder your being at peace while you wait on whatever
or whomever you are believing for

Fresh
Air to breathe while
Inhaling,
Trusting God and exhaling
Hopelessness

Formidable foe against
Anything
Insisting
That we can't
Have our hopes and dreams

19

1 and 9 = Faith

One's hope for the future

Author's notes:

My faith in Papa God now is not contingent on whether I believe He is real or believe Him to be a promise keeper. But my faith now is in "I know" that He is real and a faithful promise-keeper. He stirs my faith and faithfulness with the remembrance of every promise kept.

Faith, Faithfully: I agree to trust

First
Acknowledging God has given all that
Is needed
To live a prosperous and successful life
Here on earth

Faithful: Loyal

Faith-filled: Full of faith to agree and cling to until it happens

Faithfulness: Being shown to be reliable

***Loyal:** Faithful in allegiance

Loyalty: Being there for someone through the highs and lows, staying by their side regardless of the circumstances. It involves accepting and loving someone for who they are, without threatening to leave them when things become challenging.

***Trust (ed, ing):** An assured reliance on the character, strength, or truth of someone or something

Taking a
Risk with
Understanding
Somethings
Take time before what you want or need is brought
to light

⚜Trustworthy: Able to be relied on as honest or truthful

Believe: To accept as true.

Bringing thoughts into an agreement to
Embrace something as real, even though it may not
Look as
If it should be
Embraced. But an inner sense seems to
Validate the
Earnest ability to receive it as truth.

Belief: Confident trust in specific facts; knowledge

Basically
Embracing knowledge from experience or teachings,
Letting it be what will be used
Indiscriminately, without further thought, and then
Executing actions that were
Founded by deep-seated acceptance of what was planted, to what is right or wrong

***Convince (d):** To bring (as by argument) to belief or action

Depend on

Decision made to take
Expectations and
Put them on things and people to
Enter into agreement to fulfill
Needs looking for
Displays that

Openly can be seen to meet
Needs and grow trust

Peace: At rest during a situation. Rest assured.

Purposefully
Engaging in
Accepting being
Cared for by God,
Even when it doesn't make sense

PEACE
↓
I AGREE TO TRUST

Unifying Fruitfulness

1 and 9 = A unique fruitfulness

Unearthing of our
Need for each other's
Individual uniqueness,
For it is in our
Yielding to and
Insisting
No one should be forced to
Give in to

Falsifying who they
Really are, that true
Unity can
In any way, be achieved
To
Further
Understand to
Love is to
Not
Exclude anyone which
Successfully
Sews us together where anything can be achieved.

20/Twenty

The number sign speaks of

What once was and can be again

Even if

Nothing points to it being possible, but the

Truth is, anything is possible if

You only believe and trust God to help you bring it to pass.

Redeem (s), Redemption, Redeemed, Redeeming, Redemptive

***Redeem:** To ransom free or rescue by paying a price; to free from the consequences of sin; to remove the obligation by payment; to convert into something of value; to atone for; fulfill

Regain possession of something in
Exchange of payment
Donated in such a way so that
Everything is covered. No one could
Ever
Make a legal claim again to what's been redeemed.

6 = Mankind's
+14 = Healing from sin is
20 = Redemption

2	**AND**	**0**	**=**	**20**
Secured	**Unlimitedly**			**Redemption**
Secured	**Absolutely**			**Redemption**

In God With God

Resolute to
Embrace what's been
Damaged in the
Effort to
Ensure
Mending and restoration to a healthy state

Recharge
Expectations to
Dynamite doubts
Eradicating
Existing lies that have
Made it hard to believe you can be free

Reel in
Ego --- Release yourself to your
Divine Almighty Nature --- God's DNA to
Embrace and
Envelop yourself in the overcoming
Mindset of the Most High to live by

Remain
Engaged in the process of
Dismantling
Evil efforts to keep someone
Enslaved to an oppressive
Mindset that there is forever-unpaid debt (with forever
increasing hidden fees)

Regaining "Dominion" over
Everything in my life by
Deliberately demonstrating what that looks like by
Entering into a time of faith-filled follow-through to obtain
Exponential
Momentum to achieve whatever God has intended to bring forth on His behalf

Restart by
Emptying and letting go, making room for
Downloads of
Education that
Enables you to
Make better decisions on how to take back what's yours that others have laid claim to

Reform by
Educating yourself on the
Details of the rights that have been
Eminently given by God to
Engage in extracting what
Maybe being held hostage, illegitimately

Redirect
Every bit of energy
Draining
Emotion (s) and
Enlist them in
Manifesting “The Take Back” plan for a “Comeback”

Rip open the
Executive orders from God to
Demand by the Power of the Holy Spirit, the release of
Everyone and
Everything
Made free by decree of the Most High God

Refurbish
Everything in
Dire need to
Establish
Entrance into a
***M**ore than enough* time for living

Revive and
Educate the
Downtrodden to be
Expectant of an
Exodus (exit) from bondage to
Mindsets of being held hostage by hopelessness

Realign your
Expectations for a
Download of
Eye-opening
Enlightenment for
Manifesting "more"

Rope in
Emotions that
Deny
Entrance of
Elevated
Mindsets that would detail your authority to take back what is yours
Reset
Expectations of what can be
Done by
Enlisting help from our
Eternal
Most High God, to repossess what's yours

Recouping losses by
Entering into a
Demarcating time or
Electing to
Embrace whatever needs to be done to
Make it plain, "I will not be denied what is mine."

Restart my
Expectations by putting a
Demand on
Effort while
Expecting and embracing grace to
Make whatever (?) happen

Regain
Everything that's in your
Dominion to do so by
Entering into a time of
Embracing the promise with a fresh grip until full
Manifestation

Recertification that
Explains the
Details of what
Exactly has been
Extracted by
Meeting the obligation, renders the debt "Paid in Full."

Rescue of
Every delayed
Dream I've
Ever had that our
Everlasting Father says it is still
Mine to have

Recover (Y): To recoup; to recuperate; to cover again

Regaining
Everything that
Could
Offer
Validation from
Evil losses and illnesses
that tried to keep
Rule over you

Reaffirming action that can
be
Emotionally
Charged and can
Offer
Victorious validation that
Encourages someone to
believe they are
Really cared about

Allow Papa God to recover you.

Regain: To recoup losses, to reach again, to recapture

Reclaim: To repossess, to retrieve, to get back.

Retrieve: To rescue, to salvage, to take back, to get back, to save

***Rescue (ed, ing):** To free from danger, harm, or confinement

***Release:** To set free from confinement or restraint; to relieve from something that oppresses, confines, or burdens; relief or deliverance from sorrow, suffering, or trouble; discharge from an obligation or responsibility; the act of setting free

Term Made Possible: 2 and 0
Sanctioned unlimitedness

Provided by: 2 and 0
Support unlimited

***Reconcile (ed, ing):** To bring into harmony again;
to bring balance

Set Apart Unlimitedly: 2 and 0, preserved to the uttermost

2 and 0
Preserved to the Uttermost
Secured Absolutely

COMEBACK

Counteraction and
Overcoming some
Monumental
Event that was meant to
Break you
And insist that you
Can't make it "over" or "through," attempting to
Keep you from believing you can

Switch Gears

2 and 0

Reset is Eminent --- Absolutely paramount in importance reengaging after a stalled situation

✟**Reestablish:** To establish again or anew
in God's "All Things Work" promise

It means...

Revenge on
Evil
Elements that
Sought to destroy you (your health, life, hopes, dreams, relationships, finances...) and
Take
Away anyway to
Believe that
Life is worth living and
Is
Salvageable with
Help from heaven

21/Twenty-One

The

Winning number to

Encourage

Networking;

The coming together and

Yielding to

Once again, treating each other as if we

Need

Each other

Redeem (ed, ing, er): Unity 20 + 1

Redeem Unity

Recover (ed, ing, er): Unity

20 + 1
Recover Unity

Regain (ed, ing, er): Unity

20 + 1
Regain Unity

Reclaim (ed, ing, er): Unity

20 + 1
Reclaim Unity

Reconnect (ed, ing, or): Rewire; re-join; recombine;
*Come back together again

Rallying cry from
Eternity and everyone who desires to
Come together again,
Opposing any
Negatives that's
Not
Encouraging
Consistent
Togetherness

***Reunion:** The state of being reunited

Secure (ed, ing) Unity: Doing whatever it takes to bring harmony

2 and 1
Secure (ed, ing) Unity

Reconcile: Join; merge; resolve; reunite; settle

"Stitched" Together

Sewn ...
Tied to one another through
Ideas, hearts, minds, and
Troubling times that
Causes us to want to
Help
Each other
Drawing us ever closer in relationships.

Sewn
Together through
Intimate
Times of
Communicating connections that
Hold up
Even when
Dire straits challenge the relationship

***Share (d, ing):** To use or enjoy with others; participate

22/Twenty-Two

This number represents the
Wonder of
Eternity being revealed in
Nuggets and outpourings
That
You can understand.

This is the
Window
Opening from the heart and mind of God to the heart and mind of mankind.

Revelation: Manifestation of light; the unhindered reveal of what was once hidden; the reveal and release of truth

***Reveal (ed, ing,):** To make known; to show plainly; open up to view

Vision: Eye-opening truth, a God-given reveal
* The power of sight; the ability to see; an image created in the imagination; a supernatural appearance; insight or foresight

Truth: The actual state of things, reality

The
Real
Undeniable
Tracing and revealing what may have been
Hidden, when uncovered, it will be found to be
"irrefutable"

Understanding: An awareness; an agreement of opinion or feeling things, concepts, or ideas that at one time didn't make sense to you, but now do.

Seek and Find

Set yourself to
Engage in
Earnestly
Knowing what something is

About
Not
Depending on others to

Furnish
Information that may
Not contain the
Depth of what you could find yourself in or what God is willing and waiting to reveal to you

***Wisdom:** Accumulated knowledge; insight; good sense

What, where, when, and how
Instructional insights granted by God to
Show and
Demonstrate an understanding to
Oversee a
Matter when needed

Where
Informational knowledge, when exercised,
Starts to be a
Demonstration of an
Overcoming nature,
Making things simple that once appeared "complicated."

Discern (ed, ing, ment): To tell the difference; distinguish; detect; to intuitively know something; the power to know things without conscious reasoning.

***Show:** To cause or permit to be seen; confer, bestow, reveal, disclose, instruct; prove

Show: Let it be seen how = a demonstrative display of how to do or what has already taken place; bring attention to

Look and Watch

Leave yourself
Open to
Observe in a
Keen (strong, mentally alert) way

Allowing
Nothing to
Distract

While waiting for the
Appearance of the
Truth
Contained within
Hidden matters

Knowing

Knowledge that
Need not be
Observed over and over, but
Within and
Instinctively,
Now is
Governed by God to be accessed whenever needed

Testimony of Authority: The telling of "authority" found while going through tests, trials, and tribulations that leaves you knowing that you're an overcomer

<u>10 + 12 = 22</u>
Testimony of Authority

The Glory Story of Authority: This is telling the story of giving honor to God for equipping, empowering, and enabling you to go through, overcome, and then empower others to know they can be overcomers as well with God's help.

<u>10 + 12 = 22</u>
Glory Story of Authority

For Such a Time as This

10	+	12	=	22
Truth		Scheduled		for Reveal

10	+	12	=	22
Appointed time				for Reveal

Hidden Mysteries: Things that are here but not understood or were not known to be in existence until now--- no reference points

Buried knowledge: Refocusing on what was once known and lost with *The Fall*

Prophetic: Revealing of things to come

Fresh Perspective: Some new way of viewing something; new angle, new take, new viewpoint

Crystal Clear Perception: Making sure there's no room for doubt; unquestionable awareness; discernment; undeniable sensitivity; sharp insightfulness

***Evident (ce):** Clear to the vision and understanding; manifest, distinct, obvious, apparent, plain; an outward sign; proof; testimony

10 Testimony
<u>+12 Authenticity</u>
22 = Evident (ce)

Enlightened (ed, ing, ment): To make clear; to be informed; to be educated; free-thinking.

***Surprise (d, ing):** To amaze; to astonish

***Instruction:** lesson; practice; guided direction; led action; the process of teaching

Avail (able, ability): To be of use or advantage; help, benefit; usable and accessible

Recognized Authority: Truth is power, and when shared, it is a notable authority established, recognized, and often acknowledged.

Recognize: Identify; diagnose; comprehend; realize

***Recognition:** Acknowledgment

⌖**Record:** To give evidence of; a thing constituting a piece of evidence about the past, especially an account kept in writing or some other permanent form

***Revise:** To look over something written to correct or improve

Real (ity, ing, ly): Unquestionable; genuine; authentic; factual; valid

Reveal of
Everything that's
Authentic and
Liveable

***Realize (ed, ing, ation):** To make actual; to be aware of

***Clarity:** Clearness; transparency

***Review:** To study or examine again

Recall by
Examining what's been
Viewed before with the
Intent to
Evaluate
What may not have been the whole of a matter

Remembrance: To revisit in thought what might have been believed to have been forgotten

23/Twenty-Three

This number
Will help you
Enter into a Right-
Now
Trust in God, where
You can know

That
He is
Ready and
Eager to let you know you are secure with Him here on
Earth.

Set Apart by God: Purposely kept in a distressing situation, that later spoke, *you needed to be there so His presence could make a difference*.

Consecrated by God: Set apart for His purposes.

Redeemed by God: He did what was necessary to bring us back to Him, leaving us with free will to choose whether or not we, in turn, wanted to be with Him.

Recovered by God: Covered again after being left uncovered/exposed to the harsh elements of life and left to fend for yourself (ourselves)

Redeeming or Recovering Power: Power used to reestablish what was once considered lost, undermined, or hindered.

Recovering Power: The ability and power to recover

Redeeming Power: The power to redeem (pay the price for whatever is held hostage until payment is made)

Testimony of being delivered: 10 + 13 = 23

Testimony of deliverance

Detailing the trials and tests before your deliverance

Glory Story of Deliverance: Dealing with now knowing how God was present and helped you become liberated during times of trouble

24/Twenty-Four

This number represents a

Witness to

Everybody who

Needs

To know that

You can have a trusting relationship with God,

Finding

Out and

Understanding He is

Ready, willing, and waiting for you to know Him.

***Relationship:** The state of being related or interrelated; linked or bonded

Family: Those you are bound to by love, blood, or both

From
A
Mindset of heartfelt
Intimacy through
Love relationships
You embrace, regardless of whether or not natural DNA is the connection

Fellowship: Communion (the coming together); the condition of the friendly relationships existing among people

Friendship: Loving, inspirational partnership between friends

Prayer: Devotions; simple conversations with God

Prayer

Place of
Releasing
All
You have,
Every concern, in "exchange" for
Rest and peace

Pure purpose-filled
Relationship with the
Almighty God that
You can
Enter into and know it's
Real and relevant for your life

Place to
Receive and release
All that's needed for
You to
Ever have
Real, lasting enjoyment and overcoming success in this life

Yoked Together: To be linked together for one purpose; to be equal

Glory Story of Salvation: 10 + 14 = 24
Story of healing and wholeness

The telling of God's orchestrated redemption and recovery of mankind for a possible intimate relationship

A Holy Creation: 24 2 and 4
Holy Creation
Set apart Creation, Sacred Creation

Love Language: Loving conversation 8 + 16 = 24

Nu Love ↕

Communication

Communicate (ed, ing, tion): To convey and/or relay
* To make known; to pass from one to another; join or connect; exchange of information or opinion

Prayer Fellowship: Sweet communion. Time spent communicating with God about the issues in both your hearts — His and yours — becomes a sweet incense of sacrificed self. Re: You sharing it with Him instead of keeping it to yourself

***Communion:** To communicate intimately

Loving New Beginnings:

16 + 8 = 24

Loving Nu beginnings of relationship

Worship: To give great high regard; to show extravagant respect and honor; to show reverence

When
Overwhelmed with the
Realization that a
Show of
Honor
Is only
Proper to acknowledge
the greatness of who *God Is*!!!
Wild
Out-of-this-world abandonment to what
Refusing
Self from
Having more say than God,
Is a
Picture of worship

When you choose Papa God's way
Over any other way,
Regardless of how much easier they
Seem to be,
He is
Infinitely
Pleased

Willingness to
Offer,
Releasing your will,
Submitting to
His will (God's), with Him being the only
Insurance you need to
Put your trust in

Willingness for His will to be
Outstretched and
Raised as a
Standard,
Here as it
Is in heaven, to
Proclaim and display God's Glory

What
Others count as insignificant when you
Refuse
Self to
Honor God
Is no little thing in your
Papa God's eyes

What looks like to
Others to be
Ridiculous to
Show
How much you are
Invested in
Publicly putting your heart on display for God and others

Warring
On behalf of
Righteousness is a
Sacrificial offering that
Honors God
In the
Purest of ways

When you
Observe the
Reality that
Someone so loving, so faithful, deserves all the
Honor we could ever give and
Insist on
Putting your love offering on display

When you're willing to
Overlook (ignore) and
Refuse to let
Situations
Hinder or stop you from
Intimately
Pressing into being present in God's presence

When the
Only
Rest for your
Soul is to give in to
Him (God)
In spite of how
People would see and treat you, rest (Be at peace)

When the
Only thing that you feel is emptiness, it's perfect to
Receive from God
Showing
Him honor by
Insisting He's the only one you trust to
Put back in what you need to be whole

When faced with
Overwhelming odds that
Readily
Screams, "There is no
Honor
In
Putting your trust in God," you do it anyway

When you find yourself
Overwhelmed and being
Rushed to make a quick decision, and you
Stop and wait to
Hear what God wants you to do, and you do it,
It's a
Position of worship (honoring God)

When
Others
Rale and
Say terrible things about God, step in and
Honor Him, even when
It's not
Popular

When it's
Obvious that
Remaining
Steadfast in your
Honoring God has severe consequences,
Instead of downplaying the relationship, you
Press into being bold like never before

What you do when it appears you're
Outnumbered and you
Realize it's time to lovingly
Summon
He who is
Invested in
Protecting and empowering you to win

What you do to
Order your thinking with
Righteousness,
So as to
Have the
Infinite
Power of God from the presence of God

What looks to
Others as
Radical
Submission to something or someone they may
Have never known or
Imagined to be a
Priority

What looks to
Others to be
Ridiculously
Shameful, but you're willing to
Have them think whatever,
Ignoring anything that would interfere with your
Perfecting praise for and toward your God

Willing to "witness and testify"
Of the
Regal
Splendor of our
Heavenly Father
In hopes of
Preparing hearts for an invitation to encounter Papa God

When you're about to walk
Out on your
Relationship with God and you
Stop to give
Him another opportunity to show you who He
Is in spite of
Painful disappointments

When you
Overturn
Reasoning and
Start to
Handle your
Imaginings that scare you by
Putting them on the altar and allowing God to arise in
your situation

When warring
Over what's
Right and you
Submit to
His way
Instead of your way is a
Precious offering to God

***Share (d, ing):** To partake of, use, experience, occupy, or enjoy with others; to have in common a shared passion

Evangelism

Love-Inspired, "Prayerful Interactions"

Prepared
Readiness to
Always
Yield your
Expectations of what you think is the
Right way
For you to interact with someone on God's behalf
Understanding that
Love must be the foundation for the

Interaction, and only God knows the
Need
That must be met first for trust of
Engagement to be possible without
Rights of the person being
Assaulted by
Careless invasions of
Those who
Insist they have the right to go places that
Only God is to have access to and
Not even God goes places in our lives without
Some kind of agreement to go. He is not a thug or rapist.
He is a Gentle God
waiting for an
"Invite."

25/Twenty-Five

This number
Will stand to remind
Everyone how
Not
To trust in only what
You think you can do, but also know, having

Faith, that
In times of trouble, God is a
Very present help for
Everyone willing to put their trust in Him.

Set Apart by Grace: 2 and five

Set apart by Grace

Reserved, anchored, and honored by Grace

Redeeming Grace: 20 + 5

Redeeming Grace

... is for when things need another chance or time to happen with the help of God, bringing back around the hope, help, and opportunity to get right what was wrong; to win and gain what was considered defeated and lost, with overlapping grace for what appears to be "done deals," impossibles made possible!

Recovering Grace: 20 + 5

Recovering Grace

The power of Grace to recover

Testimony of Restoration: 10 + 15

Testimony of Restoration

Particulars of what you went through to be restored

Glory Story of Restoration: 10 + 15

Glory Story of Restoration

The telling of how God did it

26/Twenty-Six

This number

When viewed and understood, reveals that

Everyone has a

Need to know

That

You can be

Secured

In knowing that deep down inside, you are a

Xeroxed "carbon copy" of God.

Carbon Copy

Carefully
Agreed upon
Royals (all mankind) recognizing being
Birthed--- brought forth to
Openly show how
Natural it

Can be to
Overcome anything
Put in
Your way because you have the power of the original to draw from and depend on

Set Apart Mankind: 2 and 6

To be intentionally separated for a specific purpose; all mankind being different from the rest of nature

Redeemed/Recovered Man: God orchestrated reunion with mankind.

Glory Story of Love: 10 + 16 = 26

Glory story of love

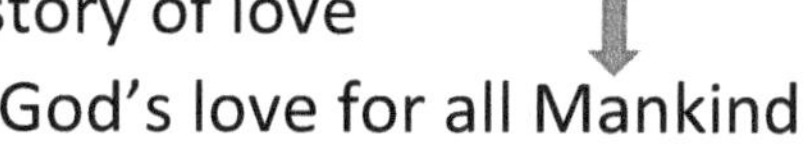

God's love for all Mankind

Testimony of Love: 10 + 16 = 26

Testimony of love

God's love for all Mankind

The telling of trials and tests that revealed God's love and care

Glory Story of Unified Man: 10 + 1 and 6 = 26

Story of Unified Mankind

Redeemed Recovered Mankind

27/Twenty-Seven

This number is the
Wake-up call to
Everyone, that
Now is
The time to
Yield to

Securing your relationship with God while you're here on
Earth,
Voluntarily
Entering a love relay, finding out He is
Not a keeper of rules; He is the keeper of "hearts."

Secured Completely: <u>2 and 7</u>
Secured Completely

Set Apart Completely: <u>2 and 7</u>
Set Apart Completely

"Seal The Deal"

Redeemed Completely: <u>20 + 7</u>
Redeemed Completely

Recovered Completely: <u>20 + 7</u>
Recovered Completely

Redeem (ed, ing): Completely <u>20 + 7</u>

- *Perfection:* To know that your *perfecting* is in Him
- *Connection:* To know that your connection to Him is sure
- *Protection:* To know that God has afforded your protection--- He has covered the cost.

Recover (ed, ing, y): Completely (ed) <u>20 + 7</u>

- *Perfection:* What threatened to stay marred *(That which is brought back into a perfected and unblemished state)*
- *Connection:* Relinking of what was disconnected
- *Protection:* Security being trusted again

28/Twenty-Eight

This number

Will

Encourage you

Not

To

Yield to lies that

Evilly

Insist

God

Has no interest or power

To help you, when the truth is, He's waiting to give you "new." Ask Him for it!!!

Set Apart for New Beginnings: 2 and 8

Set apart for Nu Beginnings

Set Apart to Become New Beings: Always evolving, becoming new 2 and 8

Set apart Nu Beings

Redeem (ed, ing) New Beginnings, New Beings:

20 + 8 = 28

Redeemed Nu Beings

Redeemed Nu Beginnings

Recover (ed, ing) New Beginnings, New Beings:

20 + 8 = 28

Recovered Nu Beings

Recovered Nu Beginnings

Testimony of The End of Bondage:

10 + 18 = 28

Testimony of the End of Bondage

Testimony of Glorious Nu Beginnings

Your story of how it happened

20 8

Take Back And Renew

29/Twenty-Nine

This number
Will be an
Eye-opening
Number
To show
You how you only

Need to call on God. He's waiting to show you how
Invested He is in meeting your
Needs
Even when you feel you don't know Him well enough for Him to do it.

Secured Future: 2 and 9

Secured Future

Redeemed Future and Recovered Future:

20 + 9 = 29

Redeemed Future

Recovered Future

Set Apart Fruitfully: 2 and 9

Set apart Fruitfully

Set apart for Life

Set apart for Future use

Secured Fruitfully: 2 and 9

Secured Fruitfully

Redeem (ed, ing) Fruitfulness: 20 + 9

Redeemed

→ Fruitfulness

Redeeming

Recover (ed, ing, y) Fruitfulness: 20 + 9

Recovered Fruitfulness

Testimony of Faith: 10 + 19

Testimony of Faith

Telling of how faith made the difference

Glory Story of Faith: 10 + 19
Glory Story of Faith

Telling of how specifically faith in God made the difference

Glorious Faith: 10 + 19
Glorious Faith

This is evident when the bright brilliance of your faith shines through. It is noticeable to those who know you are going through dark times. And when your faith shines through to light your way in the darkness, it encourages others to have faith in their dark times.

30/Thirty

This number represents God's unlimited power

Here on earth, for anyone

Interested in

Really having a

Touch from Him and willing to

Yield and be open to a real relationship with the Almighty Most High God.

God Almighty: 3 and 0
God Almighty

God Unlimited: 3 and 0
God Unlimited

Power Unlimited: 3 and 0

Power Unlimited

Empowerment Unlimited: 3 and 0

Empowerment Unlimited

Powered unlimitedly to get done whatever will increase and prosper you and others.

***Maturity:** The quality or state of being mature; full development. 30

Mature (ity)

Maturity is not a matter of age but of how you choose to respond to various life situations. It is a level of mental development or wisdom that affects all areas of an individual's life.

Raised from Obscurity: Seemingly, brought into view as if from out of nowhere. 3 and 0

Raised from Obscurity

The Redeemed Glory Story: 20 + 10

Redeemed Glory Story

The recognizing and telling of how it was in God's time and on His dime that you overcame despite your instigated loss and defeat by not always doing what you needed to do.

Redeeming Glory Story: <u>20 + 10</u>
Redeeming Glory Story

It tells of someone being redeemed from life's trials and tribulations that they overcame, emphasizing how God made it possible.

The Recover (ed, ing) Glory Story: <u>20 + 10</u>
Recovered Glory Story

The recovered understanding of God's involvement in your life through extreme challenges that enabled you to endure.

Redeeming Testimony: <u>20 + 10</u>
Redeeming Testimony

It tells of someone's life experiences that can help others know there's hope and the power to achieve the same results if the same principles used in the testimony are applied to a similar situation.

Miraculous: Things that occur outside the rules of science or natural laws.

<u>3 and 0 = 30</u>

Miracles Unlimited

Miracles Unlimited: Impossibilities made possible, happening in immeasurable and unbelievable ways.

God Orchestrated Unlimitedness: God's providential, perfectly timed reveal of His involvement in the infinite opportunities that can be embraced in life.

40/FORTY

Finds
Out what you're
Really made of. It
Tries you, grows you, presses you into increase
before transitioning
You into your greater.

Transition: To shift or move; to change over; a passage from one state, place, stage, or subject to another.

End of Trials and Testing into Transition

There have been times biblically noted where **40** marked the end of some trials and tests before transitioning into new places. One such time was when Moses was **forty** years on the backside of a mountain before being called to lead God's people out of Egypt. Another time was after the children of Israel were disobedient; they wandered around in the wilderness for **forty** years before they were allowed to enter the "Promise Land."

Noah built an Ark to survive a **40**-day, **40**-night flood, where all life, except those in the Ark, was lost. But after **forty** days, God allowed Noah and his family to land on solid ground and start again.

Jesus also fasted for **40** days and **40** nights before transitioning into His "ministry."

And then there is you. How does this pertain to your life?

Transfer: Relocation; resettlement; handover; reassignment

Create (ivity, ed, ing,) Unlimited (ly): The ability to create in immeasurable ways.

***Transform (ed, ing, ation, er):** To change in structure, appearance, or character; transfigure; alter; makeover.

Transformative Power: The energy and ability to change things, making a difference in people's lives and situations with something already established.

Life Abundantly

Life Teaming with Possibilities!!!

50/Fifty

Finally, this is the number that represents the
Incomparable, indescribable, unfathomable
Force of heaven
That is willing to partner with us if we're willing to
Yield to the truth that we need help to live this life on earth

"Holy Spirit"

The Holy Spirit's

Glory Story

10 Pictures

Of Who He Is

HOLY SPIRIT

He is

Only the most

Lovingly loyal to

You when you need Him "friend," you could ever have here on earth.

Someone who stands by to

Partner with you

In whatever

Right thing you choose to do that

Inevitably (certainly unavoidably), will

Take some power beyond your human abilities to make happen.

HOLY SPIRIT

He is always

On the alert to

Lend Himself to whatever

You may need

Seeing as how He has agreed to be

Part of anyone's life

If you are

Ready to

Invite Him into

The details of your life that need His consistent

"oversight" (supervision).

How bout it?

He's got

Super-Vision.

He misses nothing.

You can trust Him

to do right

by "you."

HOLY SPIRIT

Honorable, but seldom "honored"

Overlooked

Lover of our lives who

Yearns to be

Seen as a

Personal friend who

Is

Reliable and

In

This life with us to the end and beyond if we choose for
Him to be

HOLY SPIRIT

Hears

Our

Loudest silent cries that

You think no one cares about or knows. His

Sensitivity for you is so

Powerfully pure,

It cuts

Right to the heart of a matter, and is even ready to

Interpret God's heart

Towards you so that you can know you're never alone.

HOLY SPIRIT

He's here, but

Out of sight as

Long as

You are not interested in

Seeing Him. But once a

Personal

Invitation has been given and

Received, even though He's

Invisible, He knows how

To let you know, He's there.

HOLY SPIRIT

Holder of

Opportunities to

Learn how

You can,

Simply

Put,

Imagine and

Release

Ideas, inventions, and other

Timely things that can change the course of your life

and others' history

HOLY SPIRIT

Heat for a cold soul

On

Lonely "dark" journeys where

You can't

See or feel your way to

Peace. He will

Ignite a fire

Right

In

The midst of your situation, that lets you know
you'll be alright.

HOLY SPIRIT

He is the

One who

Leaves no one

Yearning to know God without fulfilling the need.

Simply

Put, He

Is ever

Ready to

Illuminate

The truth of who God is and who you are.

HOLY SPIRIT

Hidden in plain sight, so
Only those who desire to see Him can,
Leaving it up to whoever to decide whether or not to
Yield to

Seeking Him and giving Him
Permission to
Illuminate Himself or
Reject and continue to
Ignore the
Truth of who He is, what He has been to us, and how
much we need Him still--- who He is willing
to be just for the asking

HOLY SPIRIT

Honored friend and helper from heaven

Open to

Love and lead

You into an awesome relationship with God

So you can know how

Precious you are

In His heart, and that He's

Ready to show you that

It's a

Trustworthy relationship you can depend on

The Number for The Holy Spirit:

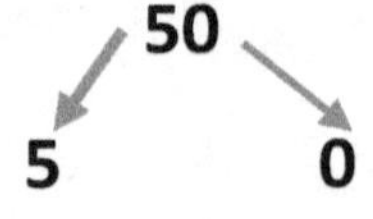

Grace Unlimited

Redeemed and Recovered Testimony: Truth told about what happened that was once shadowed by lies. Only the Holy Spirit, also called The Spirit of Truth, can help you tell the truth because He knows everything, even the things you didn't know or what you may have misunderstood or forgotten.

Redeemed and Recovered Glory Story: 20 +20 + 10
(Converting; Retrieved into value)

...is the telling of how the Holy Spirit was the only way you could know the truth, walk out the truth, and then be willing to tell the truth, regardless of what that truth may have you look like in the eyes of the "judgmental."

...spotlights the value of the once misunderstood testimony that was looked at in a degrading way, but now is revealed as a "full of the extravagant grace of God" story.

Jubilee

***Jubilee:** A special anniversary of an event, especially one that is celebrating 25 or 50 years of a reign or activity

Jubilee is an expectancy and time of grand celebration, a time to show gratitude for all God has done and His extravagant "favor" in addition to what is typically shown.

Favor and Mercies of God

Jubilee was a time for the release, liberation, and freeing of enslaved people, as well as the cancellation of debt.

Just an
Unbelievable, unforgettable time of
Being
Incredibly
Liberated to be free to
Engage and
Encounter God as being a "more than enough" God

Biblically, it was noted that special instructions were given that for every seventh year, the land and the people who farmed the land were to be given a "rest" from toil and trouble working to produce.

After seven such observances (7 × 7 = 49), the 50th year was set apart as a time of profound celebration. It was called the "Year of Jubilee" and included the cancellation of debts.

Jubilee deals with the supernatural. Every seventh year was a time for the earth to rest, and God increased the time of rest without <u>work</u>.

Found in
Leviticus: 25 (God's Redeeming Grace)

<u>2 and 5</u> Set Apart for blessing and favor
of
God's Redeeming Grace

Jubilee dealt with celebrating the supernatural promised supply while being obedient in not toiling in the seventh year to, by decree, give the land a rest, but allowing the promise of triple (Lev. 25:21 ...*"your crops shall bear forth fruit for three years..."*) amount from the sixth year to sustain until released to sow and reap after the seventh year of "rest" was observed.

The Holy Spirit

His attributes can be found in the Bible: St. John 16, and The Fruit of His Spirit in Galatians 5:22. The Holy Spirit is *The Spirit of The Most High, Almighty Creator, God,* who was left here to be so many things for us as we need Him to be. God's Holy Spirit gives life, so there's no living without Him.

- **Comforter**: He is the one who helps us to be willing to be comforted, and then He comforts us with peace and understanding, or with the peace that goes beyond comprehension when we can't come to grips with the "whys" of our situations and need that kind of miraculous peace.
- **Counselor**: He is the one who will give you wisdom and understanding so that you can make good decisions when He is asked and you allow Him to.
- **Helper**: He is the one who will help you accomplish things, even to the point of touching someone's heart to give you favor so that they can be His heart, hands, and feet to provide you with earthly help.
- **Advocate**: When you don't even know that you need help, He pleads with you to ask for help so He

can be permitted to do so. Like any good lawyer, He knows what you need and how you need it, especially since He knows everything, unlike any other lawyer.

- **Intercessor**: He is the "go-between," mediating and communicating for God and us, enabling understanding and reconciling differences, translating heart issues that are not readily known or spoken, primarily on our part. He helps arrange an understandable agreement between God and us on how to live this life and handle every earthly situation. He is the liaison of the heart and mind of God to the heart and mind of mankind and vice versa.
- **Strengthener**: When we don't think or feel like we have anything left to work with or give in the stamina department (physical, mental, emotional strength), it is He who gives us the strength to go on

One More Step
One More Day
One More Minute
One More Moment
One More Anything at a Time,

especially during chaotic times in your life when you're left spent and confused about the next steps you may feel incapable of making. He is there to "strengthen" you. Just ask Him.

- **Standby**: He is by your side when no one else can or wants to be. He is there to be your friend, guide, or someone to lean on—someone who never tires of hearing from you or hearing about what you care about. He's on standby to step in and give you what you need whenever you need it. Humans may get tired, bored, insensitive, irritated, angered, or simply unavailable. The Holy Spirit is not like that. He is always around. You just need to get to know what His presence feels and looks like. He's there waiting to be asked to reveal Himself. He's there waiting for an up-close and personal relationship you can depend on when you can't rely on anything or anyone else. He is committed to being with you until the END.

Comforter

Comes close to
Offer you whatever you
May need to
Fend
Off overwhelming feelings of sadness, grief,
disappointment, or hurt
Regarding
Times of trouble to help you
Endure until
Relief can be had, and healing can take place

Counselor

Connection to
Our conscience to give
Us understanding of what may be
Needed with decisions and actions
So that situations and circumstances
Eventually can be successfully addressed while we
Learn how to
Operate out of God's wisdom for
Righteous living

Helper

He is the
Ever-present when you need Him
Loving lifeline that, when given
Permission, will
Enter into your situations in life and help you
Realize all that is possible to be done with His help

Advocate

An agent of help who
Demonstrates caring
Voluntarily with the
Only motivation is to
Call people's
Attention
To the "love" of our
Everlasting and loving heavenly
Father,
our
Papa
Daddy, God

Intercessor

Is a mediator who helps you
Navigate your
Trust and
Emotions to
Rely on the
Caring of God where you
Elect to give all your problems to Him.
Show God you trust Him by
Submitting to His
Overwhelming peace-filled
Rest while whatever is being worked out.

Intercessor

Is the one who helps with the
Negotiations of heart-
To-heart situations that need
Evaluation for eventual
Reconciliations and prayers of agreement that
Can bring about
Effectual
Solutions to
Situations that seem
Out of our
Reach by ourselves

The Holy Spirit allows us to know Father God and communicate with Him in ways no man can explain. He is the embodiment of heaven, the ability to know, not just believe, but to know God is real.

Strengthener

Someone who
Takes the time to
Really
Encourage you to
Never
Give up even
Through
Hard, hellish, hurt-filled
Experiences that would insist you could
Never really survive or overcome. His
Encouragement comes with the embraceable power to
Rise above whatever you're faced with.

Standby: One who can be relied on, a person ready to help

Standby

Someone who, when
There is a need,
Angles and anchors Himself
Next to you, so when you need Him to
Be whoever and whatever,
You can trust that He will be there

Convicts

Cuts through the confusion that "compromise"
Often brings, regarding
Not seeing wrong and evil for what they really are,
Viewing things according to "true"
Intent instead of
Convincing yourself
That truth is
Something you can manipulate and still call it truth.
That's a lie, so He helps you to choose truth.

Convinces

Comes to
Open your eyes to what's true and honest, so you will
Not be willing to
Violate your good conscience and
Involve yourself in believing what is
Not true, so you
Can be
Encouraged to
Submit to doing what's right

Convicts but never condemns

Condemnation

Causing some-
One to believe that there's
Not ever going to be a chance to change.
Damning them to believe that
Evil is
More powerful than the power of God's love
Negating their
Ability to
Trust God would accept them, leaving them to believe
It is impossible to be delivered from
Overwhelming, oppressive,
***N**ever can get it right*, mindsets, so I might as well continue to do wrong since I have no way of ever getting it right.

He is Not a Condemner

- **Condemner:** Points out your wrongs and leaves you feeling it can never be made right (That's of the enemy).
- **Convictor:** convicts of what's not right but gives you a desire, a hope, and a plan to get it right with His help. He is a convictor of what's wrong. He makes you aware so that you can choose to do right.

The Holy Spirit is Your Good Conscience

- He is the discerner of knowing.
- He is the One who makes that part of us possible.
- He is the One who grants the ability regardless of who else is claiming and taking the credit.
- He is the Spirit of Truth and the revealer of truth.
- He is the revealer of the true nature of things.
- He equips you to deal with deceit and to have continual help to stand in truth when those around you would encourage, attempt to seduce, or even demand that you do otherwise.
- He is the revealer of God.
- He is the embodiment of God's reality.
- He is the Spirit of Truth and will lead and guide all into truth who want it.
- He tells whatever He hears Father God say and will announce and speak of future things to those with a relationship with God.
- He is the revealer of all things.

Why Should You Care About The Holy Spirit?

Well, because He is the One who gives us the ability to breathe, move, think rationally, communicate, etc., to name a few things essential for being alive. It is He who gives us the ability to do everything. This is why it is important to know Him and to partner with Him regarding your decisions concerning how you will use this gift of life.

The HOLY SPIRIT

He is the Holy, "high on loving you," help from heaven's presence of God, who is here to help us live. The Holy Spirit is the power-filled presence of God. He is

Omnipotent (All-Powerful)
Omniscient (All-Knowing)
Omnipresent (Everywhere at the same time).

He is Spirit, invisible to the naked eye but can be felt, and the evidence of His presence can always be found. By holy agreement, He agreed to stay here and do everything possible to help everyone live the "best life" they could live, righteously and in harmony with God and man, to the extent His help is allowed. Due to mankind's "free will" gift from Father God, who gave each of us to use as we saw fit, the Holy Spirit will not go against anyone's free will. But He lovingly and patiently waits to be invited into each person's life in the measure that He is asked to be there. He will not go any further than each person agrees for Him to go.

God is perfect in His intent and precise in His design of all things, leaving nothing to chance. The only things He has made room for are our "free wills," which He allows us to have and use without His control. But our heavenly Father is Omniscient (All-knowing), so He knows thoughts, intents, and choices of actions before we think or do them.

His presence ensures that any life could be lived here on earth. He is the One who has revealed to man everything we now use to live a life of ever-increasing knowledge.

When the words were spoken to create creation, the Holy Spirit was He who brought it forth from the invisible realm into full view for all to see. He is waiting to show up when invited, and He enjoys revealing anything that will help you get acquainted with or remember heaven, our home.

There is a neglect of acknowledgment of Him, even though He helps us do the simplest things. Breathing is the most taken-for-granted ability for those who have never really had problems or challenges with it, and are not able to do it. And yet, even though He is not acknowledged most of the time, He continues to supply these everyday monumental, "must have it to live" things.

Because He is so lovingly humble and never promotes Himself, He leaves it up to His friends to talk about Him if they choose to. Since He and I are friends, there is no way I could not acknowledge Him since He is the One who gave me the revelation of Father God's heart to write and display for all to benefit from the content of this book.

He is the miracle-working power of heaven on earth. He waits for those who agree with Him to partner to speak, declare, decree, and proclaim what miracle is needed and then be the instrument to bring it forth from heaven into the earth.

What Sets The Holy Spirit Apart from Other Spirits?

What makes Him considered to be Holy?

What are spirits? They are real entities, but invisible unless the personality or properties of any particular spirit are known. Example: the spirit of lying or the spirit of anger. Although spirits can be very influential, it is still an individual's choice whether to yield their free will to be used or inhabited by whatever spirit may be present—evil controlling spirits "press" people to allow them to have their way and stay.

The Holy Spirit is different from other spirits. He is **HOLY**.

Have
Only the best that
Love can provide for
You

Highest measure
Of
Love that consists of truth and righteousness
You can depend on

Holds the
Only pattern and power for
Living life where
You don't have to worry about being discarded,
for He is lovingly righteous

The Fruit of His Personality

Galatians 5:22

Love, joy, peace, kindness, goodness, self-control, patience (long-suffering), gentleness (humility), faithfulness

The Holy Spirit calls out for an invitation after you've encountered, experienced, or have been told of His goodness. He consistently operates with the highest integrity and truth, always righteous and always motivated by love.

Why it's Important to Know The Holy Spirit

Every person has been created with and given God's Spirit. This being true, it allows us to engage, encounter, and be influenced spiritually. This ability to be influenced is still governed by the "free will gift" God gave everyone, so you can choose who you allow to influence your life.

We are spirit beings and are open to the spirit realm, which makes us vulnerable to being influenced in our thinking, feelings, and actions by whichever spirit we yield to, whether with or without the knowledge or on purpose, for there are many spirits in this world today. They influence the way we think, what we say, and what we do. Spirits of anger, hatred, perversion, greed, lust, and more are out there. Still, there is no other spirit greater or equal to the Holy Spirit of God and the fruit of His personality (love, joy (gladness), peace, patience (even temperance), kindness, goodness (benevolence), faithfulness, gentleness (meekness, humility), self-control (self-restraint) that influences our personality if we let Him.

When we practice and exercise these, for the sake of it just being the right thing to do, we are allowed to see the Holy Spirit's influence in our lives. You might have believed you were just like this on your own. But do understand that in a world given to self-righteous self-centeredness, you are not doing this out of your righteousness.

When you decide to do right by refusing the fear of "I don't want to look different," know that God's Holy Spirit is giving you what you need to stand and be giving and caring. Corrupted human nature tends to be "it's all about me."

James 1:17A states, "Every good and perfect gift is from above: it comes down from the Father."

The fruit of His Spirit is a gift to be enjoyed and shared. No other spirit you may encounter has His character. Some spirits attempt to mimic the fruit of the Holy Spirit, but their true nature will be revealed when tested by their motivations. Everything done by the Holy Spirit comes from love and God, who is love.

This is to help bring awareness of whose spirit you may be keeping company with, and whether you want to continue after discovering the differences between the spirits.

He Understands Your Spiritual Need to Know

In a time when everyone is being inundated with the supernatural, paranormal, spiritual, new age, and witchcraft practices, everyone has different beliefs. The truth is that people are becoming more aware than ever that there is more to be experienced regarding the "spirit realm."

We must remember that we are part spirit beings and human beings. As a result, it is our spirit part that, to some degree of interest, ranging from fear to acknowledging those truths, that we are most curious about. Perhaps even craving to be connected to the supernatural in some way. But without knowing the seriousness of not understanding that taking an interest in studying the things mentioned above encourages one to leave oneself open to evil, unsafe spirits. And becoming friends with them because of promises of enrichment is dangerous.

You may be unaware that you are giving, without boundaries, permission for those spirits to infiltrate your thinking and actions. They can take over your personality and convince you that the changes were okay and that you made them. Their invited presence in your life can bring about devastating consequences such as depression, anger issues, and an increased need for control. Deep feelings of the need to be isolated as your spiritual senses are assaulted and terrorized, and even broken relationships, loss of finances, and deteriorating mental and physical health, to name a few. But the Holy Spirit is the loving, truth-filled revealer regarding the supernatural spirit realm. He is the safe link to spiritual, "safe-for-your-soul" encounters that edify, leaving you feeling more loved and accepted with a clearer understanding and a greater sense of God's nearness to you: God cares for you. Freely He gives. Your investment is the time you spend receiving from Him.

Number for The Holy Spirit

Grace Unlimited: 5 and 0

God's
Release of
All that's needed for us to
Care for ourselves here on
Earth- it's for whoever wants and needs it and is willing to ask Him for it

Unfathomable depths grace can reach, and the unbelievable lengths grace will go to meet a
Need to show what the
Love of God looks like beyond
Imagination leaving
Many doubting because
It often makes no sense when you
Think about how, at times, there has been doubt cast that you could
Ever really have a
Direct line to God. But the Holy Spirit is our direct line.

You have the power to change your life when you embrace the truth. God gave us “dominion” over life here on earth. Let your number messages empower you with God’s word for your situations and for what you can experience in the future. Get His word for you, then let it “RIP.”

You are the **prophet** over your own life (destiny). Get with the Omniscient One (all-knowing). Hear what His word is for you. Embrace it, open your mouth, and let it “Rip.”

Person who
Reveals what
Often is
Partially
Hidden to
Encourage
Taking hold of
promises and wisdom for direction--- Anything that can help prepare us for our futures

Proclaims your future success by
Releasing the
Overcoming
Prosperous word
Heard when your
Eyes
See what God would say to
You about your life.

During the writing of this particular topic, these number messages came to me:

<u>1044</u>

Gloriously creating and building a

<u>31</u>

God orchestrated unity for a

<u>1115</u>

Guaranteed restoration to our whole identity of being

Him in the earth

Made in His image and likeness with power from within

to speak and create with the power of our

WORDS

Make no mistake or be deceived; know that everyone houses God's creative power, and their thoughts, words, and actions produce something positive or negative daily. We all have been made in the image of the Almighty One. And just as He spoke His intentions into reality when He created the whole of us, we all have the power to do the same. Question? What are you creating with the spoken intentions of your words? Why not allow God, by His word to you and His grace-filled Holy Spirit, to help you get locked into only releasing what you want and not anything you don't want? You should often embrace, proclaim, and repeat what He tells you as the truth of your present and future.

There is a scripture from the Bible that says, and it is true, Romans 10:17 (A glorious testimony of victory), *"So faith comes from hearing and hearing by the word of God."* Let your eyes help you to listen, and then take it to heart, and let the power of your tongue

release your promises

calling them into existence.

Fill your heart and mind with His promises, and then speak.

Matt. 12:34: For out of the abundance of the heart, the mouth speaks.

Luke 6:45: A good man brings forth good things from the good stored in his heart.

Proverbs 18:21: Life and death are in the power of the tongue, and they who love it shall eat of its fruit.

What fruit are you producing and eating to bring forth what you want?

LET IT RIP!!!

The number **"12"** stands for "authority," and the number **"3"** stands for "God." Take the authority (12) of God (3), which equals fifteen ways to let it "Rip" to enforce the truth that God never intended for another to have more say over your life than He and you. Regain, release, and reign (rule over) / rain (shower, saturate, and soak) in His word for your life.

Why let it 'Rip'?

- Plan of action for your faith in your future
- Rest in knowing God's gotcha, so do your thing.
- Awake every morning knowing you have "Nu" (New unlimited) mercies.

Your steps are ordered, and His grace is sufficient even when you get it wrong. His grace is superabundant and available to help you "get it right."

Release the
Instruction filled
Plans for your future.

Replay the
Instructions for giving yourself
Permission to move into action.

Recapture and
Implement your
Promise to trigger the release of the power of His word to you.

Reveal and repeat the
Intricate details often of what your
Promise will look like from what God tells you is coming.

Reset your expectations by
Investing in
Periodically speaking your promise back into view.

Rebuild an
Inner confidence by
Prophesying (speak forth).

Rejoice
In knowing your
Promises are on the way.

Reestablish
Inner
Peace from your promises being constantly on your mind.

Redefine what
It looks like to believe in your
Promises.

Reconnect with the
Images of your
Promises.

Rely more
In the
Providential hand of God in the ordered steps of your future.

Rest
In knowing your
Promises are **scheduled** to happen.

Remember the
Importance of the
Promise.

Reassure yourself whenever
In doubt that your
Promises will come to pass.

Redo and renew your mindsets by
Investing in
Purposefully “breathing” new life into your situations by speaking a reminder of your promises.

The Solar Eclipse Identity Chart

Years ago, I came across this chart, and because I had reservations about using it due to past teachings, God let me know it was okay after asking Him about it. He gave me the explanation, which I will share with you shortly.

I wanted this to be one more weapon to combat "identity crises" when we sometimes feel down and need encouragement and a reminder of how uniquely extraordinary we are. Have fun finding out how you "glow in the dark." The greatness is in you, and it's time to see it.

Get
Lies
Out of the
Way and start to embrace the awesomeness of who you are.

Doubts that
At times, try to
Rule you, and
Kill off your knowing that you are "more"

Solar Eclipse Identity

Who are you when the sun's light (SON) has been blocked out with clouds of dark doubts?

Use the Day of Your Birth

1-5	6-10	11-15	16-20
A Creator	Ruler	Guardian	Oracle

21-25	26-31
Angel	Seeker

Use the Last Number of Your Birth Year

0	1	2	3
Of Powerful	Of Cosmic	Of Divine	Of Limitless

4	5	6	7
Of Sacred	Of Radiant	Of Profound	Of Spiritual

8	9
Of Radical	Of Magnificent

YOUR ZODIAC SIGN

Use Your Zodiac Sign

Aquarius	**Jan. 20- Feb. 18**	**REVOLUTION**
Pisces	**Feb. 19- Mar. 20**	**VISIONS**
Aries	**Mar. 21- Apr. 19**	**PASSION**
Taurus	**Apr. 20- May 20**	**PLEASURE (Fun)**
Gemini	**May 21- June 20**	**IDEAS**
Cancer	**June 21- July 22**	**COMPASSION**
Leo	**July 23- Aug. 22**	**STRENGTH**
Virgo	**Aug. 23- Sept. 22**	**EXCELLENCE**
Libra	**Sept. 23- Oct. 22**	**PEACE**
Scorpio	**Oct. 23- Nov. 21**	**MYSTERIES**
Sagittarius	**Nov. 22- Dec. 21**	**TRUTH**
Capricorn	**Dec. 22- Jan. 19**	**WISDOM**

******[This information was found online with no declared author.]***

What And How You Think And Believe

Titus 1:15 AMP:

"To the pure (in heart and conscience), all things are pure, but nothing is pure to the defiled, corrupt, and unbelieving. Their very minds and consciences are defiled and polluted."

There have always been great debates about how much we should care about the stars and space in life's everyday living. Some religions, like Christianity, have frowned upon astrology, horoscopes, and zodiac signs as nothing but evil that has nothing to do with God. Yet, since the beginning of time, God has allowed humanity to use the stars as navigational tools for adventurers, explorers, and seamen.

If you knew how to navigate the road patterns of the stars and constellations in the sky, you could always keep on track here on earth to get from one place to another.

In Matthew 2:2 of the Bible, there is an account of how the Three Wise Men were able to find Jesus. Being led by a star, they navigated their way and found Him. Bible prophecy (foretelling of what's to come) indicated that The Wise Men were astrologers from the East. Astrology, in and of itself, is the science of how the stars speak of things to come and is not evil. It becomes a corrupt practice when astrology is used wickedly to control people in their day-to-day lives, with them trusting in it alone. It's about what and whom you worship and why.

Science is needful. God grants man understanding to help, but things get off keel when man worships and believes that what they know of science is more significant than its creator. That's when God has a problem with this practice. It is not with astrology but the worship of astrology.

Three "Need to Know" Balances In the Sea of Positivity Regarding Numbers

2 11 13

The above title was given to this section to draw attention to the fact that, among the numbers defined in this book, three numbers are sometimes used to highlight situations of a dishonorable nature. All three deal with mindsets, heart conditions, and motivations.

The first of these numbers is the number "2." This number in the Love Language book means many honorable things, such as *holy, sacred, set apart for honorable purposes, secure, anchoring, and honoring*. And yet that same number can carry meanings of *dissension, disrespect, dishonor, division, divisiveness, segregation (made or forced to be separate), and disunity (separation through discord)*.

The first set of meanings deals with respect, love, and caring. The second set addresses the lack of respect, love, and caring, where divisive hatred can thrive.

When dealing with your personal communications, God can and will emphasize and spotlight which of these words and their meanings pertain to whatever is being addressed. He will let you know the true nature of a situation and whether any involvement or active participation should be agreed to. He will clarify what should be stood for or against regarding His will for the situation.

The second number under the title is the number "11." This number has many meanings related to *advocacy*.

Absolution
Justification
Justice
Validation
Vindication
To cover and keep,
and mercy, just to name a few... but this number can also sometimes stand for *injustice,* which creates a need for righteous "judgment."

Injustice: The violation of a person's rights, unfairness, an unjust act or deed, wrong.

Instances of infractions of
Not
Justly
Utilizing
Some degree of fair
Treatment that would
Indicate a lack of
Caring and respecting of
Everyone, and not a chosen few

Righteous Judgement

Release of an
Indictment that
God
Has allowed to
Tell of the
Evil that has
Obviously gone
Unchecked for
Sometimes that has

Jeopardized and
Undermined
Determined safety and moral
Guidelines to keep
Everyone safe
Making it imperative that some action must be
Executed to
Now, put a stop
To what has been deemed as wrong and unacceptable

God does not give permission or support to anything He would not do. He is a just God and a loving Father.

The third number is the number "13." This number also has several different meanings, but the two that will be addressed here are

Rebellion
vs
Deliverance from.

Rebellion has always been perceived to be only something evil. This is true when it deals with someone rebelling against righteous laws and statutes that were put in place for safety and order to protectively dissuade or arrest those who cause hurt, harm, danger, bring confusion, or utter chaos--- a state in which nothing could prosper or last for long with any real quality of life. But then there is *deliverance.*

The need for deliverance results from having to fight, resist, or rebel against being made to submit to things, situations, and even laws that have been put in place so that certain people groups can rule over others. They unrighteously cover and give passes of non-accountability for those in power and authority or those connected to such groups while demanding harsh treatment for those who are vulnerable, disrespected, and disfavored by them. Then, the need for a fight against unrighteous rule may become necessary. Those on the opposing side will see it as an act of evil rebellion. These are ego maniacs, deceived and drunk with power, who demand submission regardless of the unfairness of their abusive rulership.

The first deals with "I want." And so, I am willing to break the rules and laws to get my way, regardless of how it may affect others.

The second concerns securing a quality of life and survival from oppression. This includes escaping fatal repercussions when those in some authority believe they have the right to enforce their will to kill those who refuse to submit.

Rebellion is resisting to submit to anything that goes against what you instinctively know is right in God's eyes and the **holiness** of His heart.

His
Overwhelming
Love and care that
Is
Noted by His
Establishing for everyone a
Standard of the utmost, pure integrity that can be
Submitted to

Resisting submitting to laws to govern actions and behaviors that do not lend themselves to the betterment and safety of all, but concentrate on "self," is the definition of rebellion. But deliverance from evil injustice is backed by God.

God is love.
God is truth.
God is perfect and balanced, and He wants us to know the difference when something is not.

TIME

The
Incremental
Measurement of
Eternity here on earth that's not needed in heaven,
helps humanity to stay focused
and intentional, a gift to help us
until we get back home to perfect
"unlimitedness"

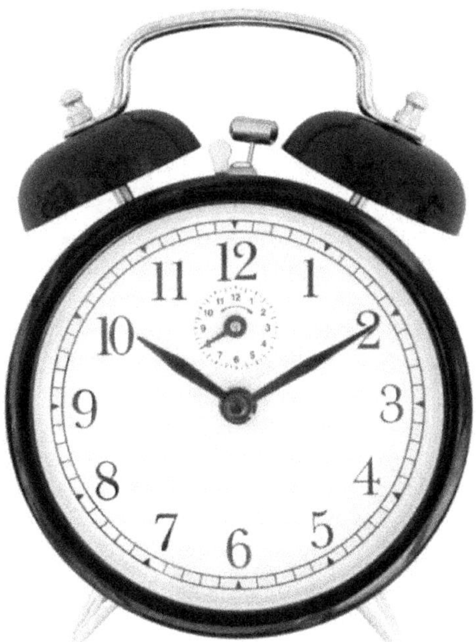

God's Reminder from the "Clock"

Who He is every day, twice a day

God is

111

The only One who can do the impossible

The only One who knows all about everything without explanation

The only One whose love is so "unconditional," He has given us free will to say no to Him and not fear immediate reprisal, as you could have from telling some power here on earth "no."

God is

222

He is the
Overall
Life-form, and should be
Yielded to as being "The Sovereign God,"

Supreme being
Over everything,
Vast
Eternal
Ruler over
Everyone whom He has
Invested in
Giving of Himself so we could be the very
Nature of who He is

High
On
Loving
You

Highest in
Observing "righteousness"
Leading by example so
You and I could follow and "reproduce"
a right standard
here on earth
as it is in
heaven

God is

333

All-Powerful

The Resurrector of dead things that, by purpose, need to live again

The Empowerment for others to be able to do the same

God is

444

The Creator of all things good and perfectly perfecting

He is creativity.

He is the giver of creativeness.

God is

555

Gr8er Still Grace … Gr8er Still

I chose to use the number "8" in the word "Gr8er" to emphasize that by His grace, we can always have "new beginnings." However, remember that whatever amount of grace is needed to achieve peace and prosperity in and on your journey here on earth is always available.

Heaven is a place of peace, unlimited and without interruption. All things stay Nu (New unlimited) there, but here, it's Gr8, and comforting to know that in…

Lam 3:21-23

"But this I recall and therefore have I hope and expectation; It is because of the Lord's mercy and loving-kindness that we are not consumed because His {tender} compassions fail not. They are new every morning; great and abundant is your stability and faithfulness."

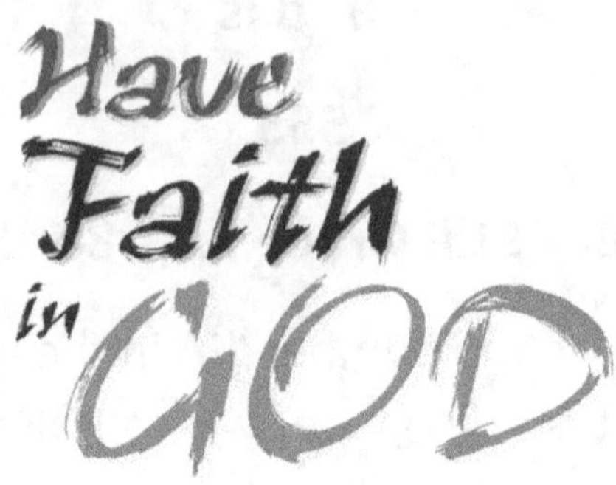

GOD IS

	All-Power	All-Knowing	Everywhere
0	Omnipotent	Omniscient	Omnipresent

1 The one true living God

2 Holy, high on loving you, God

3 He is the one who was and is and always will be resurrection power, God.

4 Almighty Creator of us all, God

5 He is the gracious, kind, merciful help for all who need and ask for Him, God.

6 He who is found in the midst of mankind, God

7 He is perfect and a perfecting God.

8 He is the renewer of life—The God of new birth.

9 Author of life, God

10 Great and glorious God

11 The just, merciful, and forgiving God

12 Almighty authority over all, God

13 A delivering unifying, empowering God

14 Saving and healing God

15 Restoring God

16 Loving God

17 Victorious—more than enough, God

18 Bondage breaker—freedom assuring God

19 Faithful God

20 Redeemer—recoverer of all things that have been lost or stolen, including "time," God

21 Redeemer—recoverer of unity, God

22 The Revealer of all things, God

23 Consecrating God

24 Author of relationships, God

25 Redeeming grace, God

26 Redeemer—recoverer of mankind, God

27 Redeemer—recoverer of our perfected state, God

28 Redeemer—securer of Nu beginnings, God

29 Redeemer of life, God

30 God Almighty—unlimited God over everything

40 Transforming God

50 The number for the Holy Spirit of God—Grace Uunlimited

All Things in Life

All things in life worth living add up to Him being in it

The Holy Spirit

HE IS:

0 + 50 = 50 Unlimited in grace in unlimited ways

1 + 49 = 50 The One and only creator of life

2 + 48 = 50 Distinct creator of all things new

3 + 47 = 50 The power of God to create and perfect

4 + 46 = 50 Creator of the creativity of mankind

5 + 45 = 50 Grace that builds us up and leaves a blessing

6 + 44 = 50 Mankind's creative ability

7 + 43 = 50 The perfecting, correcting, connecting, protecting, creative power of God

8 + 42 = 50 Nu-life and beginnings created and secured by Him

9 + 41 = 50 Future created for us by Him

10+ 40 = 50 Glorious creating of everything by Him

11+ 39 = 50 Guaranteed, God orchestrated future

12+ 38 = 50 Authority and empowerment to start again

13+ 37 = 50 Delivering power of God to perfect whatever

14+ 36 = 50 Freedom and empowerment to be whoever you were meant to be

15+ 35 = 50 Rest (peace), and God granted grace

16+ 34 = 50 Love that has the power to create

17+ 33 = 50 Victory God orchestrated, and God powered

18+ 32 = 50 Breaking of bondages and God-given security

19+ 31 = 50 Faith in God to be One with Him
20+ 30 = 50 Recovery of all God has for us is unlimited
21+ 29 = 50 Redeemer of unity or reunion to be secured for the future
22+ 28 = 50 Revealer of what's been "held in trust" for Nu beginnings
23+ 27 = 50 Redeeming power to secure change
24+ 26 = 50 Prayers answered for the redeeming of all mankind
25+ 25 = 50 Redeeming grace to set apart and bless
26+ 24 = 50 Redeemed mankind made secure by the creator
27+ 23 = 50 Distinct connection to the redeeming power of God
28+ 22 = 50 Securer of "Nu" (never seen before) and revealer of the truth of it
29+ 21 = 50 Securer of the future fruit-filled reunion with God and man
30+ 20 = 50 The miraculous, unlimited redeemer makes the impossible possible
31+ 19 = 50 God orchestrated unity with faith, and Him showing us how
32+ 18 = 50 God securer and breaker of bondages for glorious Nu beginnings
33+ 17 = 50 God orchestrated empowerment to bring forth victory
34+ 16 = 50 God's creative power to unite all mankind with love

35+ 15 = 50 Power-filled grace to bring about rest and restoration
36+ 14 = 50 The power for mankind to be healed and saved from himself
37+ 13 = 50 Power to perfect, correct, connect, and deliver
38+ 12 = 50 God orchestrated Nu beginnings, and the author of the timings
39+ 11 = 50 Power to preserve life and to be satisfied
40+ 10 = 50 Creator of unbelievable testimonies (glory stories)
41+ 9 = 50 Creator of unity and fruitfulness
42+ 8 = 50 Creator and anchoring source for Nu beginnings
43+ 7 = 50 Creative power who perfects, connects, and protects
44+ 6 = 50 The creative creativity of mankind
45+ 5 = 50 Transformative grace to bless
46+ 4 = 50 Creative ability of mankind to create
47+ 3 = 50 Creative perfecting power
48+ 2 = 50 Creator of Nu (never been seen before) held in reserve
49+ 1 = 50 Creator of the future for us
50+ 0 = 50 The Holy Spirit is unlimited in every way, especially grace unlimited

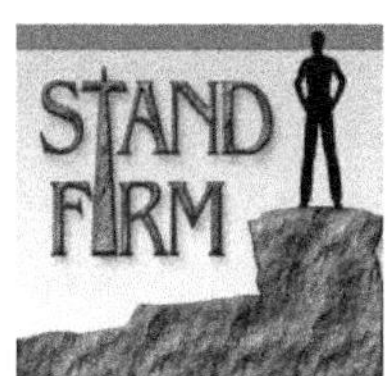

Grace, You Can Trust

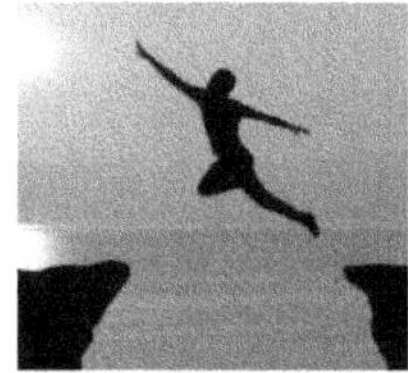

How He Still Sees You

How all the numbers add up to how your
Papa Creator, God created you to be,
and how He still sees you,
despite all the layers of lies that say
"You are not"

These are just a few examples, but for those really into numbers and math, I know you have so many more equations that will be fun to break down and see how you're the one in the equation with all your awesome "unlimitedness."

0 1 1
0 + 1 = 1 The unlimitedness of you uniquely displayed

1 0 1
1 + 0 = 1 You being seen as unlimited and one-of-a-kind by Him

0 2 2
0 + 2 = 2 Absolutely (without a doubt) set apart to be different

2 0 2
2 + 0 = 2 Set apart to be unlimited in a distinct way by Him

0 3 3
0 + 3 = 3 The unlimitedness of God in you = miracles

3 **0** **3**

3 + 0 = 3 The power of God unlimited and miraculous

0 **4** **4**

0 + 4 = 4 Unlimitedly created in the creator's image

4 **0** **4**

4 + 0 = 4 Created to be unlimited just like our creator

0 **5** **5**

0 + 5 = 5 Unlimitedly graced to be a blessing

5 **0** **5**

5 + 0 = 5 Blessed unlimitedly to be gracious

0 **6** **6**

0 + 6 = 6 Unlimited mankind includes us all

6 **0** **6**

6 + 0 = 6 All of us absolutely means all mankind (not a chosen few)

0 **7** **7**

0 + 7 = 7 Unlimitedly connected to perfection if we want Him (God is perfect)

7 **0** **7**

7 + 0 = 7 Connected unlimitedly to Him, the perfect ONE

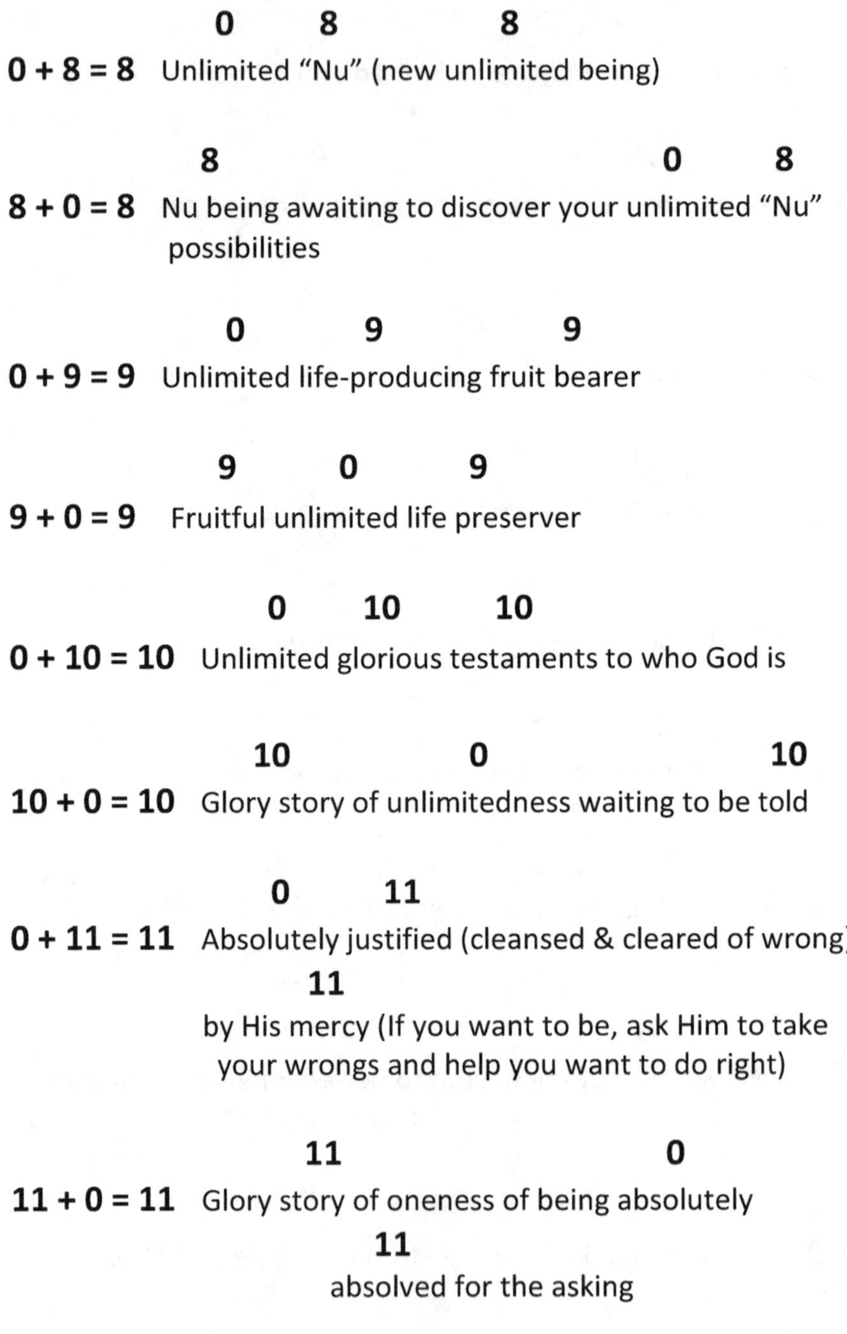

0 8 8
0 + 8 = 8 Unlimited "Nu" (new unlimited being)

8 0 8
8 + 0 = 8 Nu being awaiting to discover your unlimited "Nu" possibilities

0 9 9
0 + 9 = 9 Unlimited life-producing fruit bearer

9 0 9
9 + 0 = 9 Fruitful unlimited life preserver

0 10 10
0 + 10 = 10 Unlimited glorious testaments to who God is

10 0 10
10 + 0 = 10 Glory story of unlimitedness waiting to be told

0 11
0 + 11 = 11 Absolutely justified (cleansed & cleared of wrong)
11
by His mercy (If you want to be, ask Him to take your wrongs and help you want to do right)

11 0
11 + 0 = 11 Glory story of oneness of being absolutely
11
absolved for the asking

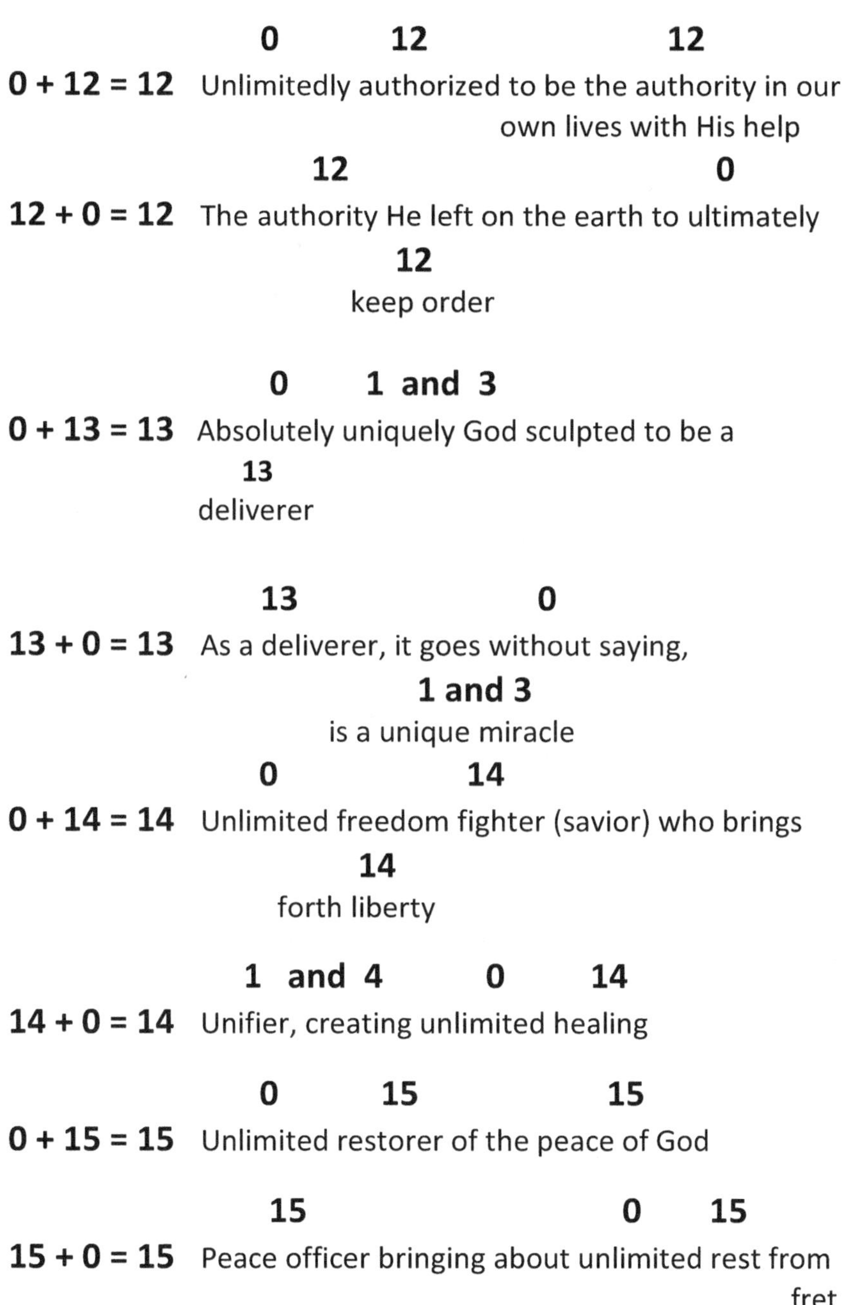

0 12 12

0 + 12 = 12 Unlimitedly authorized to be the authority in our own lives with His help

12 0

12 + 0 = 12 The authority He left on the earth to ultimately

12

keep order

0 1 and 3

0 + 13 = 13 Absolutely uniquely God sculpted to be a

13

deliverer

13 0

13 + 0 = 13 As a deliverer, it goes without saying,

1 and 3

is a unique miracle

0 14

0 + 14 = 14 Unlimited freedom fighter (savior) who brings

14

forth liberty

1 and 4 0 14

14 + 0 = 14 Unifier, creating unlimited healing

0 15 15

0 + 15 = 15 Unlimited restorer of the peace of God

15 0 15

15 + 0 = 15 Peace officer bringing about unlimited rest from fret

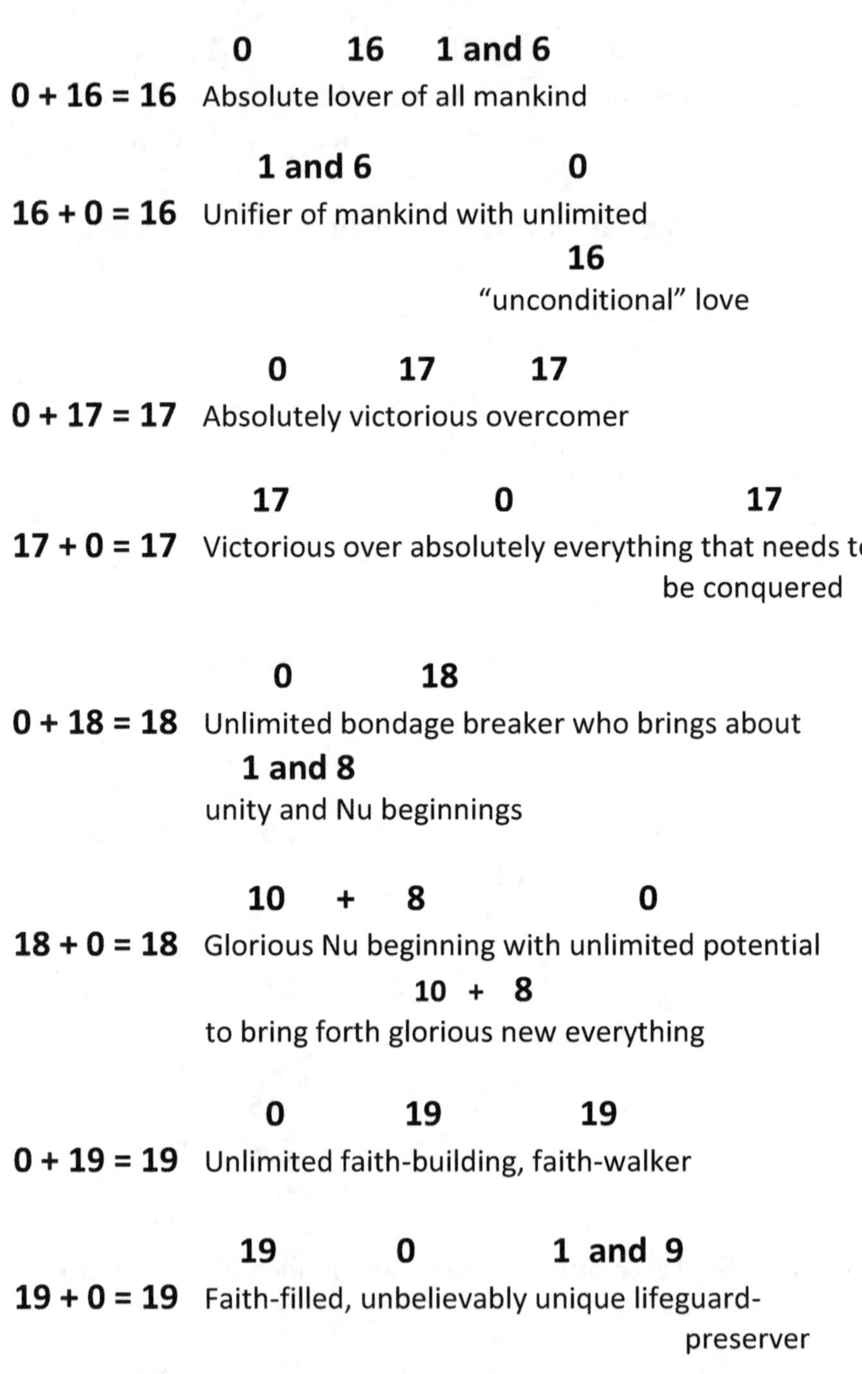

0 16 1 and 6

0 + 16 = 16 Absolute lover of all mankind

1 and 6 0

16 + 0 = 16 Unifier of mankind with unlimited

16

"unconditional" love

0 17 17

0 + 17 = 17 Absolutely victorious overcomer

17 0 17

17 + 0 = 17 Victorious over absolutely everything that needs to be conquered

0 18

0 + 18 = 18 Unlimited bondage breaker who brings about

1 and 8

unity and Nu beginnings

10 + 8 0

18 + 0 = 18 Glorious Nu beginning with unlimited potential

10 + 8

to bring forth glorious new everything

0 19 19

0 + 19 = 19 Unlimited faith-building, faith-walker

19 0 1 and 9

19 + 0 = 19 Faith-filled, unbelievably unique lifeguard-preserver

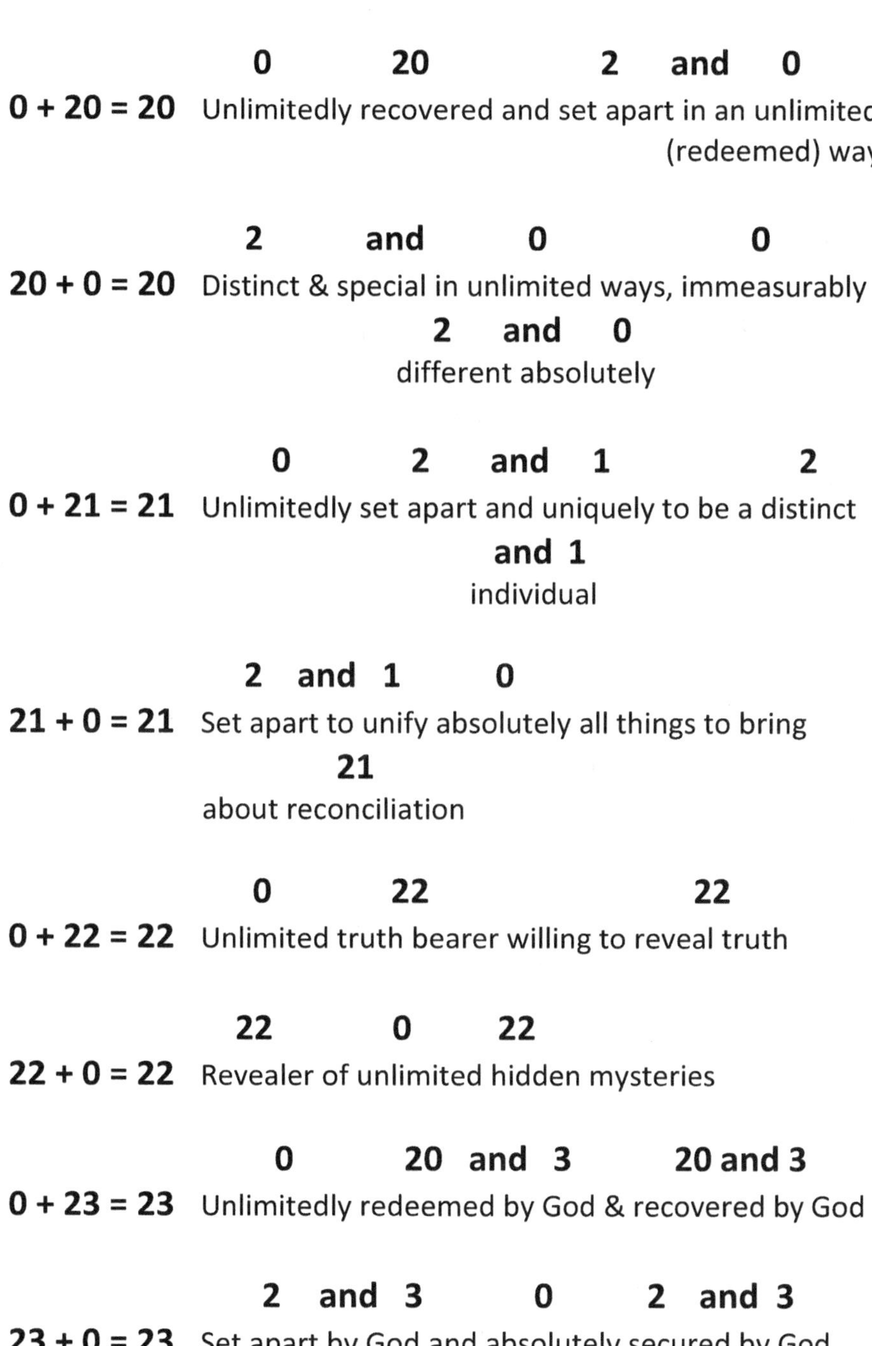

0 20 2 and 0

0 + 20 = 20 Unlimitedly recovered and set apart in an unlimited (redeemed) way

2 and 0 0

20 + 0 = 20 Distinct & special in unlimited ways, immeasurably

2 and 0

different absolutely

0 2 and 1 2

0 + 21 = 21 Unlimitedly set apart and uniquely to be a distinct

and 1

individual

2 and 1 0

21 + 0 = 21 Set apart to unify absolutely all things to bring

21

about reconciliation

0 22 22

0 + 22 = 22 Unlimited truth bearer willing to reveal truth

22 0 22

22 + 0 = 22 Revealer of unlimited hidden mysteries

0 20 and 3 20 and 3

0 + 23 = 23 Unlimitedly redeemed by God & recovered by God

2 and 3 0 2 and 3

23 + 0 = 23 Set apart by God and absolutely secured by God

24

0 + 24 = 24 Absolutely made to have a relationship of

16 + 8 = 24

loving Nu beginnings for fellowship

2 and 4 0

24 + 0 = 24 Set apart to create absolutely anything that

2 and 4

supports creation

0 25 2

0 + 25 = 25 Unlimited redeeming grace that anchors people

and 5

with favor

25 0 2 and

25 + 0 = 25 Redeemingly graced and absolutely set apart to be

5

a blessing

0 20 and 6

0 + 26 = 26 Absolutely redemption is yours and

20 6

recovery is yours

20 and 6 0

26 + 0 = 26 The redemption of all mankind ultimately

2 and 6

secures you

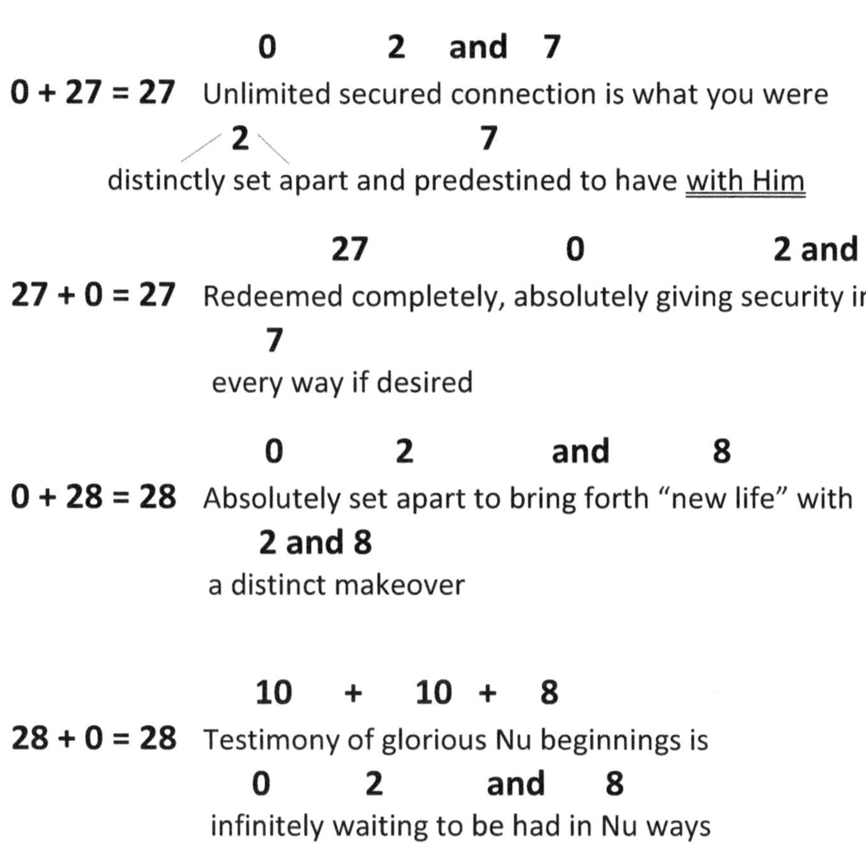

0 2 and 7

0 + 27 = 27 Unlimited secured connection is what you were

2 7

distinctly set apart and predestined to have with Him

27 0 2 and

27 + 0 = 27 Redeemed completely, absolutely giving security in

7

every way if desired

0 2 and 8

0 + 28 = 28 Absolutely set apart to bring forth "new life" with

2 and 8

a distinct makeover

10 + 10 + 8

28 + 0 = 28 Testimony of glorious Nu beginnings is

0 2 and 8

infinitely waiting to be had in Nu ways

0 2 and 9 2

0 + 29 = 29 Absolutely set apart fruitfully for a secured

and 9

prosperous life

20 and 9 0 20 and

29 + 0 = 29 Redeemed future of unlimited redeemed

9

fruitfulness (regardless of your age)

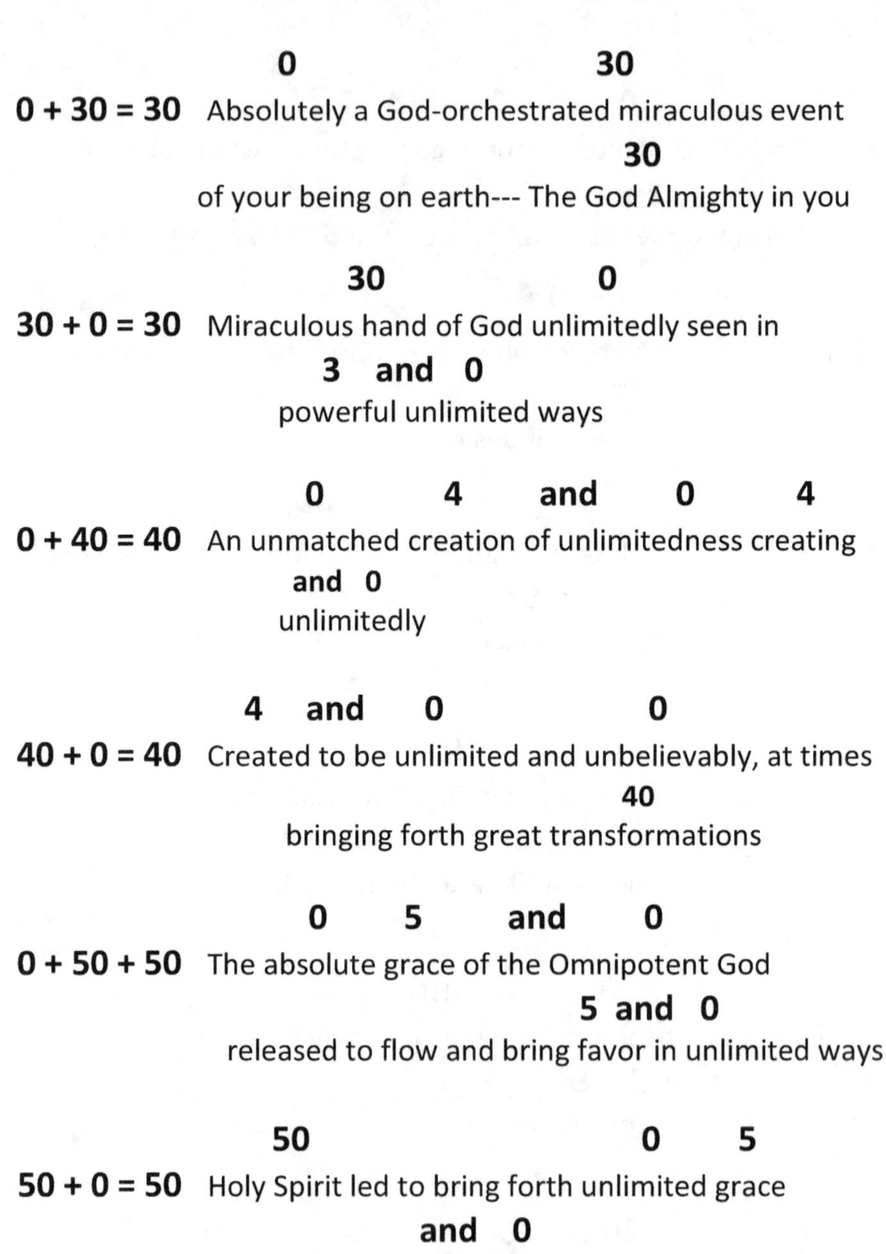

0 **30**
0 + 30 = 30 Absolutely a God-orchestrated miraculous event
30
of your being on earth--- The God Almighty in you

30 **0**
30 + 0 = 30 Miraculous hand of God unlimitedly seen in
3 and 0
powerful unlimited ways

0 **4** **and** **0** **4**
0 + 40 = 40 An unmatched creation of unlimitedness creating
and 0
unlimitedly

4 and 0 **0**
40 + 0 = 40 Created to be unlimited and unbelievably, at times
40
bringing forth great transformations

0 **5** **and** **0**
0 + 50 + 50 The absolute grace of the Omnipotent God
5 and 0
released to flow and bring favor in unlimited ways

50 **0** **5**
50 + 0 = 50 Holy Spirit led to bring forth unlimited grace
and 0
in unlimited ways

God sees all these things and so much more when He looks at us. He sees past our human parts and all our faults. God sees our God parts made in His image. If we want to see and experience Him, we only need to ask that God reveal Himself in us because He's in there. Time to agree for Him to arise and come forth in your life. Your part is to make room.

Let go of all the things that could

Negate
Receiving
Embracing
And
Manifesting your "true identity."

Negatives to Positives

When you believe that your life is operating in the negative and that no number message can lift you, guess what? God specializes in turning negatives into positives.

0 = 50 When you feel you have nothing and no one, the Holy Spirit can reveal to you that with Him, you have more than you think you do.

-1 = 50 When you feel all alone, He is the One who's there to be whoever you need Him to be.

-2 = 50 When you are feeling ostracized for being different, the Holy Spirit can reveal how your difference was given to make a difference.

-3 = 50 When you may feel like you have no power, and God couldn't possibly be with you, He promised He would never leave or forsake you. He is ready to show you your "I Can" can outweigh your "I Can't" with His help.

-4 = **50** When you believe you lack
ability to be all you were created
to be, the Holy Spirit can show you
what a "wondrous creation" you are…
designed with the ability to create.

-5 = **50** When you've been made to believe
you are cursed and not blessed,
allow the Holy Spirit to reveal
how blessed you really are.

-6 = **50** When it feels like you're nothing and
all mankind is against you,
again, the Holy Spirit can and will be
what and whom you need
but, He also knows where
those you will fit in with, are.
Ask Him to reveal and bring
those relationships together.

-7 = **50** When you've been told repeatedly
how you can and will never get
anything right, the Holy Spirit is waiting
to help you get whatever you need right.

-8 = 50 When you believe you will
always be stuck in the same old
place with the same old trouble,
get with the Holy Spirit so He can show
you what "Nu" you can have
if you follow His lead.

-9 = 50 When life doesn't seem worth
living, if you ask Him, the Holy Spirit
will reveal how that's not true. There
is more life waiting to be lived.

-10 = 50 When it seems you can't get a sign,
a testimony, or any other kind of
help, believe the best is yet to come
if you hold on. Breathe. Be still and
ask for a sign and an adjustment
of your sight to see it. Often,
signs are misunderstood or hidden
in the blindness of your pain. Ask the Holy Spirit
to erase that pain and open your eyes.
*"Weeping may endure for a night. But
Joy comes in the morning."*

-11 = **50** When it appears that there are no
justice, mercy, or forgiveness in your life,
turn to the Holy Spirit to give you what
you need to help you hold on
until the change comes.

-12 = **50** When it appears as if everybody
but you have authority in your life,
allow the Holy Spirit to teach you how
to practically take power and the
authority God gave you to live your life.
Take it back. Stand up and execute
your free will to bring about what's
best for you.

-13 = **50** When it appears to be no way out
of a situation and no way to make it better,
the Holy Spirit will help you learn how to navigate
safe comings and goings to bring about
the deliverance that would get you restarted
into the expanse of your future.

-14 = **50** When it appears there's no freedom
to exercise your free will,
contrary to the lies--- there is.

-15 = 50 When it seems you can't get any "rest," the Holy Spirit can be your resting place.

-16 = 50 When you are feeling "uncovered" and unworthy of love, the Holy Spirit is waiting for you to spend time with Him because in His presence those oppressive feelings can be washed away by the power of God's loving presence, which is who the Holy Spirit is.

-17 = 50 When fear and failure seem to be the only companions who choose to stick close to you, the Holy Spirit can empower and show you how one step at a time in the right direction is the victory that overcomes all fears of failing if you refuse to stop counting everything as a negative and start seeing everything as the next step. The challenges are strengthening you so that you won't crumble under the weight of your *greater*.

-18 = **50** When you feel as if you are in chains, and negativity can never be broken, the Holy Spirit is a "chain breaker." He has the power and can empower you to go through what you need to be free, introducing you to a "Glorious Nu" beginning.

-19 = **50** When you feel you have no faith for hope, the Holy Spirit will comfort and console you if you allow Him to. There are times He will partner with others to come along beside you, but there are other times when you may feel as if no human can understand the depths of your pain. The Holy Spirit desires you to ask Him to reveal Himself to give you what no person can. He can and will if you want Him to.

-20 = **50** When it appears that no redemption or recovery could ever apply to your situation, the Holy Spirit can bring about both, if you depend on Him, and then ask Him to show you

how to walk that out in your
everyday life.

-21 = **50** When it comes to broken relationships, and it appears that all hope is lost, the Holy Spirit is a mender of the broken-hearted and a repairer of bridges for those who desire to be reconciled (brought back together).

-22 = **50** When confusion is the darkness in which you live when it appears no truth can be found, the Holy Spirit is the revealer of truth. He shines a bright light to reveal truth to those who desire it. And then empowers us to walk in truth, when the demand of the day is that we live lies to be accepted and not challenge that which is wrong.

-23 = **50** When you feel exposed and uncovered, ask the Holy Spirit to "recover" you. He is doing it already, but ask Him to help you feel Him there.

-24 = **50** When you've been told and
treated like you are a creature;
a less-than-God creation,
the Holy Spirit can reveal that
you are a "holy creation" who
God loves to hear from. He
waits to talk with you and spend
time with you until your "fraudulent,
mistaken identity" is stripped, and
you come to know yourself as the
apple of His eye--- the heartbeat of His heart.

-25 = **50** When it appears it's too late
to change things for the better,
the Holy Spirit can help you believe in
"redeeming grace" that causes
what seems like "done deals"
come back around so that
you can take advantage now
having the wisdom and desire to do
things differently; this time, righting any
wrongs. Only God/Holy Spirit can
do that for you. It would be as if
He turned back the hands of time.

-26 = **50** When it seems as if the
world and mankind are in

a devastating state--- no real
good or lasting positives, the Holy Spirit
can help you be open to believe
that not everyone is out to do wrong.
Be willing and open to believing
that positives in the world can
begin with you. You have the power
to prove that things aren't all bad.
Be a positive example.
It can start with you.

-27 = **50** When you have been repeatedly
left uncovered and left alone
fending for yourself, feeling
detached from everyone, you see
yourself as so "flawed," and that there
is no hope, the Holy Spirit can help, and
is there for the asking. He can help
you become "assured" that you are covered.
You can be as connected as you
want to be with God. You can
be assured of the truth that
God is perfect already and
He can clothe you from the inside out
if that's what you desire. Just ask.

-28 = **50** When you are sure that it is
impossible to have Nu beginnings
because *fill in the blank*, the Holy Spirit
can show you how nothing is
unattainable, and Papa God has secured
Nu beginnings for you. The only
thing is that you need to be
prepared to let go of the old
to make room for the "Nu."
He knows how hard this can be.
The Holy Spirit is present to point out
what's old and useless,
and then help you let go.
He can bring about your Nu
even giving you "Nu sight" so you
can recognize the difference.
And He will strengthen
you to get it done,
leaving you with a testimony
of bondages being "broken," and your
"Nu" coming into view.

-29 = **50** When it appears everything is
out of your control and your current
perceived hopelessness regarding
your future holding any hope
for dreams of promises being

fulfilled can come true, the Holy Spirit can show you that there are more in store for you than you know. He can adjust your perception regarding your only seeing yourself in a deficit position because of what or who you may be measuring your life up against, and then fire up your hope that the best is yet to come. He is holding it "in trust" for you until you can have the wisdom and wherewithal to handle the increase for your future.

-30 = **50** When it appears God is nowhere to be found, everything is dead or dying, and it seems that there's nothing--- not one thing you can do about it, the Holy Spirit is able and willing to introduce to you the experience of the super natural miraculous resurrection and retroactive power, which will cause you to increase your maturity of knowing God is always the answer for what looks "impossible."

-40 = **50** When you feel stuck in a place of
no growth, as if no changes could
ever happen, and it appears to be no
end to the trials and the testings of life,
the Holy Spirit can bring about whatever
changes are needed. He is whom you look
to help you free yourself from stagnating
situations and helping with the transformation,
and transitioning into Nu beginnings.
Ask Him to help, and then rest
in knowing He will take you at a
pace that you and He decide is best.
The accelerating agent
is to “trust Him”
from a crawl
to
baby steps
to
walking
to
running
to
giant leaps of faith, which are
all there, ready for you to get
started toward your greater.

-50 = **50** When it seems to be an absence of
any kind of grace from your
broken-hearted viewpoint of **grace**,

God is
Ready to give
Anybody but you assistance
Causing you to believe
Evil things about God and how He sees you,

the Holy Spirit is willing and able to prove you
wrong. He awaits to show you
that God's unlimited grace extends
to all who want and need it.
The Holy Spirit has been keeping you when
you didn't understand what grace
looked like for your individual
life situation. But if you're
ready to experience the grace, ask
the Holy Spirit to be and do what
He has joyously agreed to do---
reveal to you who God is and
what grace is.

How Much He Cares and How Often

Interestingly, 60 is the number used to measure time.

60 seconds = a minute
60 minutes = an hour
6 = mankind
0 = unlimitedness

God is overseeing every second of our existence. It used to be impactful to be in awe when you spoke of that being every nanosecond, but how mind-boggling with the newest measurements known is the “zeptosecond.” A zeptosecond is the shortest measure of time ever detailed by scientists thus far. It is the time it takes a light particle to cross a hydrogen molecule. That time, for the record, is 247 zeptoseconds. A zeptosecond is a trillionth of a billionth of a second or a decimal point followed by 20 zeroes, and a “1” = 0.000000000000000000001.

God cares about every “zeptosecond” and every *minute* detail of our lives. Time is not a governing factor or principle in heaven. It has been given to mankind to help him be more focused and intentional about what’s important. How much time were we willing to spend once we came away from being governed by the forever-eternal-immortal status we once had when we decided to go a different way in our reasoning? Yet, the mercy and grace of God are available every zeptosecond of our stay here on earth if we want them. You're already living by His grace and mercy, sometimes unknowingly. But when you come into agreement that you know, and you can specifically ask where you want grace and mercy to show up for you, you'll be blown over by what you now can have just for the asking. He is the help you can depend on, for there is a scripture in the Bible that states God does not slumber or sleep.

He is Omniscient, which means He knows everything. He knows things before they take place. So, without discussing having faith logically, it makes sense to go to the direct source to get the truth about anything worth knowing. He is Omnipresent, meaning that He is everywhere at the same time. Know that He is there, whether you can see or sense Him. So, ask Him to reveal Himself. Then watch for things you know couldn't have happened without divine intervention, and start a glowing, growing relationship with the One who loves you more than life as you know it. Let the time you spend with Him tell you how much He loves you.

The Loving Messages that Kiss Me to Sleep And…

The loving messages that await to kiss me into full awareness that He's always here and near, there and everywhere I need Him to be for me

Overseeing every step and
in those steps, He has provided
for every situation, good, bad, and
ugly, that may come my way with
Whatever I'll need;
Strength,
Wisdom,
Help of all kinds,
Favor,
Finances, and
Peace for the trying times that our psyche threatens to
"**wig-out**" and not come back.
Chaotic situations say I'm
here to stay, and it's nothing
you can do about it.

Wild out with worry
Imagining that there is no way,
Given the circumstances that
things could ever work out
right
Only seeing and
Understanding
Things through the view of what's not possible

Remember, we've experienced these types of threats before. But when we turned to God, He showed us that we could endure while His answer to our problems can be revealed, embraced, and executed by Him and us, all the while revealing who He is as well as who we really are---just like Him in the depths of our spirit waiting to be uncovered, discovered, viewed, reviewed, and celebrated

AS THE I AM THAT I AM

IN THE EARTH.

HOLY SPIRIT IS – Just Ask. He's Waiting

1. For those who have never heard of Him…

   You may never have heard of Him or know His name, but He sure knows about you. He knows everything about you. So, hopefully, with you knowing this and all you may have become aware of, you will have now read about who He is and whom He wants to be for you, and it will pique your interest in meeting Him.

   Just ask. He's waiting.

2. For those who have heard of Him but have not yet become acquainted with Him, maybe you would like to change that after discovering more about Him. He's available and desires to become more personal with you.

   Just ask. He's waiting.

3. For those who have become acquainted with Him but have not sought after or ever shown any interest in having a relationship with Him, you may have seen or experienced His presence and know what's possible regarding being in a relationship with Him, but for whatever reason, have not sought to solidify the relationship.

Just ask. He's waiting.

4. Those who are "fair-weather friends" only need to look Him up when there is some new desire you want to be fulfilled, and after you get what you want, you put your relationship on the back burner of life…

It is an excellent time to think about how you would feel and how hurtful it would be if that kind of treatment were afforded to you. What if someone treated you with gross disrespect and then expected you to keep being available? If this is the case, you may now want to take this time to apologize and ask Him if you guys can start over.

Just ask. He's waiting.

5. For those who had a relationship but, due to some disappointment or misunderstanding, felt He should have done more for you but didn't, you have counted Him out of your life. May you come to understand that just because things didn't turn out the way you may have wanted, it didn't mean that Papa God's Holy Spirit was not there with you in the situation. He was there, and since you're still here to tell your survival story, it is proof that He was. May you reconsider coming back into an active, intentional relationship with Him. I can say to you that He misses you.

Just ask. He's waiting.

6. For those who want a relationship with Him, but through religion, you've been convinced that you can't have it unless you jump through all these religious hoops you couldn't possibly do or keep up with, so you have accepted this relationship is only for a chosen few.

That would be a LIE. The Holy Spirit is only waiting for you to ask Him. Ask the Holy Spirit of God to reveal Himself. Ask Him to give you some evidence that He's real. Ask Him to open your spiritual eyes to see He's a gentleman waiting for an invitation.

Just ask. He's right there waiting.

7. But for those who know Him, love Him, and can't get enough of talking to Him and talking about Him, this will be another opportunity you can take advantage of to thank Him for being who He is. Still, even more, who He is to you "personally." Only you know what it's like between the two of you.

So, help me celebrate Him. We can do this by being willing to share with those unaware of all the beautiful things He does out of love, even the everyday things people often take for granted. And since you know how He stays in the background, let those who may not be aware know who made it possible, and tell who did it —the Holy Spirit. He is the One who brings all things into the light that were hidden from our knowing that they were always there. He was always there.

It is Him
the Holy Spirit of
our Father God in heaven.

Proof of the Sovereignty of God

While writing this book, I had many testimonies regarding listening and hearing while reading a message about life and our present situations.

9/29 I had such an occasion. I was lost in thought about the chaotic mess tearing at the fabric of our world. But for me, it's especially serious about watching what was destroying America —whose name is the United States; it is anything but "united" as a whole.

Whenever things bother me, God will often let me hear a piece of music in my heart to address where I am and answer the discouragement with encouragement that all is not what it seems. *"I am the I Am in the midst of the situation, waiting to be invited in to be all you need Me to be."* On this particular issue with the state of the world —my world—the United States of America, every possible -ism that could divide us was on the rise and being displayed.

God is sovereign, and nothing is by chance. Nothing is by chance! Everything that happens in life is intended by someone or something. God knows all and has placed everything to be revealed within time for some purpose; there are no coincidences. Everything has a scheduled time to show God's omniscient sovereignty, "The Great I

Am." This is true regarding the number messages that show up at just the right time to clarify questions and challenges in life when you need to know them most. God not only clarifies questions but also gives answers when needed.

The following are testimonies to show what that may look like, so you, too, can look forward to Him showing up in any number, revealing a special personal message just for you.

For example, the **ISBN** (International Standard Book Number) I assigned to my ***Black and White Paperback*** book, which I had no control over, matched the book's content and its intended purpose.

978-1-967205-51-6

9= Powered filled
7= Connection through
8= Nu (New unlimited)
1= Unity
9= Fostered and provided for
6= Us with
7= Perfected
2= Assurance that
0= Absolute unlimited
5= Grace is
1= Uniquely
6= Ours from LOVE **(1 & 6 = 16)**

The ISBN (number) message given to me for these particular numbers matched the content and purpose of this book, showing that only God can take things that seem so happenstance and reveal how He is in it from the beginning to the end.

The Difference Between A Testimony vs. A Glory Story

Both hold the power to encourage, empower, set the stage, and charge the atmosphere for miracles. But it all depends on who is doing the telling and where the emphasis is placed. The maturity and level of intimacy can govern where the focus is regarding the person's tests, trials, tribulations, or God.

They both tell an eye-opening story of His love, care, and revelation of how He wants you to see who He really is and who you really are, and the gratitude for surviving and thriving when you understand what you gained far outweighs the pain.

Testimony is telling your story, regardless of what it may look like —good or bad, successful or not; it is preciously worth telling. A testimony talks about or can speak of how you discovered you were stronger than you ever thought you could have imagined.

But a "Glory Story" is your testimony in the key of worship and how God was in it from start to finish. It speaks of how His "glory" — His character, humility, wisdom, grace, and mercy — has been left to permeate, resonate, and reside, so that you can now be a beacon of light for lost souls, leading and guiding them to God, who is love. Your Glory Story inspires worship-filled devotion when you know how much He cares.

What God's Humility Looks Like

He
Understands and refuses to
Make anyone
In any way, follow Him,
Leaving
It
To
You to take your "free will" and follow your heart, even if it doesn't include Him.

Testimony

The telling of
Events that in
Someway made a difference in your life and the
Tests and trials, along with everyday living, that
Insightfully, now can be viewed as a
Much-needed eye-
Opening
Necessity for
Your growth and maturity

Glory Story

God's
Love light
Overwhelmingly and overcomingly
Revealing how
You were never alone in your

Situations,
Tests, trials, or tribulations, but tell how
Obliviously unaware you may have been
Regarding what more was gained despite
what was suffered that leaves
You now to know you are greater than
before, and it was all because of God.

Testimonies of How He Speaks

Many, many, many testimonies of how Papa God's *love messages by numbers*, literally can be
Lifesaving
Peace restoring
Way making
Encourage boosting
Direction giving
Educational
Mystery revealing
Joy-provoking and fun for any and everyone.

Classifications of the different areas of life

(1) Spiritual
(2) Physical
(3) Natural
(4) Mental
(5) Emotional
(6) Relational
(7) Financial
(8) Opportunal (Opportunities in need of wisdom for possible participation for gain)
(9) Recreational

All the above demonstrates how "awesomely" relevant and accurate the Love Language by Numbers book has been and will forever be for those who choose to use this communication form to hear and experience "God's loving heart" in every situation life's journey presents. Through everyday conversations, crises, and even for fun, you will find that the numbers book can be a helpful tool. A variety of numbers can include numbers found from game points from your favorite games, numbers from TV and/or movies, and even the number of an episode, all matching the content of the storyline.

Each following testimony will be identified by which category or classification, whether one or more from the above list.

1.

(Mental, Emotional)

During the preparation of this book, I had a heartbreaking experience relocating some of my other manuscripts to complete electrical work in my room. The valuable manuscripts that the Lord had dictated were nowhere to be found. I assumed they had been lost after searching for hours, then days. I couldn't find them anywhere. I looked high and low, trying to locate them to no avail. I even searched the garbage outside, fearing that someone might have mistakenly thrown these documents away. The abundance of notes within this batch of paperwork could have filled five or more of my future publications. I considered what I had been given from God very precious, and since I don't type, the person who transcribes and keeps my computer files had not yet been given this information to record and back up. I was heartbroken. What had been lost was my only copy. I became heartsick because I knew God had shared His heart with me, which was so special. I couldn't shake the feeling of devastating loss. These writings represent conversations that arose while I was navigating challenging life lessons — whether through hardships or everyday life experiences —with my family, friends, and myself.

The most recent writings were many of what had been compiled over seven weeks of solid daily documentation. Anxiousness sat in because I couldn't understand what may have happened. I couldn't believe it! Papa God started letting me see the numbers 22, 4, and 18.

Revelation
Creating
Glorious Nu beginnings

I sensed, through my anguish, that God was acknowledging that He could restore to me what appeared to be permanently lost. I knew that, with the number 18, Papa said the situation was glorious and that there was great grace to start afresh. However, I still couldn't seem to shake the 'shoulda, woulda, coulda.' That's when God showed me 511 twice and then the number 6.

5 = Grace
11 = Forgive (ness)
6 = Me

5 11 6
Message = Grace to Forgive Myself
He was telling me to let it go. Don't dwell on what seems to be gone. I asked Him to help me do it, and He did.

The journey of a thousand miles must begin with a single step.

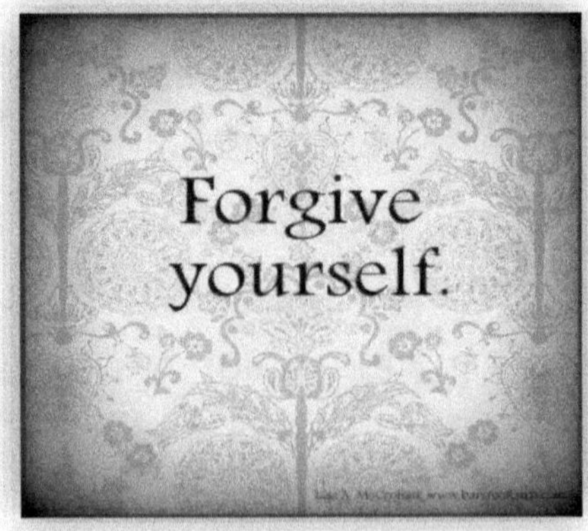

I got a sense that He was assuring me not to fret. It wasn't a loss because he would do it again, just as He had given it to me before. Remembering that the revelations were from Him, He could give me back "verbatim" precisely how He initially gave them. His number message encouraged me to believe what He promised would come to pass.

P.J. Jefferson/Author

2.

(Mental, Emotional)

Once, while being rushed to the hospital by my sister, a car came around the corner and got in front of us. They started creeping and slowed to a crawl. Anxiously, I hoped they would turn onto another street. As fear started trying to take hold, I looked at the license plate, where a message through the plate's numbers let me know that God had me in this situation. What started with me potentially becoming fearfully angry now became a private joke between God and me. If that driver had not crept and crawled, I wouldn't have been able to read the license plate number. Instead of panicking, I was able to smile my way to the hospital, reassured by the assurance that *"all things work together for my good."* The entire experience served to remind me of God's "faithfulness."

P.J. Jefferson/Author

3.

(Physical, Mental, Emotional)

Shall I Testify: In October of 2020, after suffering a heart attack a year before, I began to write a memoir concentrating on becoming a lot healthier mentally, especially physically. Additionally, I have been diagnosed with a "drop dead" disease called hypertrophic cardiomyopathy (HC). I was a 5'4" female weighing 222 pounds at that time. The extra pounds troubled me mentally and placed additional physical stress on my heart. Having HC causes the enlarged wall of my left ventricle to impede blood flow to my body. I needed to pay attention to the extra weight that magnified the strain on my heart. After a "yo-yo" battle with my weight over the past year and a half, on January 8th, 2022, just after the Thanksgiving and Christmas holiday dishes, I was back where I had started. I want to share a page from my book, “Curves, Too Flabby To Embrace?”, after discovering the spiritual meaning of numbers in a book my company helped publish by Evelyn “P.J.” Jefferson.

Excerpt from my Curves book

*[My BMI (Body Mass Index) is back up to **38**, which is morbidly obese again on the chart. On the scales, I weighed in at a visually disgusting “**222**,” back where I started a year ago. So, what next?*

*In addition to being somewhat disappointed by what this meant for my physical body, those numbers reminded me of a recent book by my sister, Evelyn “P.J.” Jefferson. That book gives the spiritual meaning of numbers like no other book I’ve ever seen; “A Love Language from the Ageless One Through Numbers.” The number “**2**” means securing in that book, and the “**22**” means revelation or vision. Those numbers can mean different things at different times. Her book is not complicated, but I suggest investing in it and studying the fascinating love language. In my situation, “**222**” tells me to “**secure my vision,**” which is precisely what God revealed to me differently. It’s good to have confirmation. By the way, the “**38**” (BMI) spiritual meaning is “**God orchestrated new beginnings.**” And since I had to start all over literally, that declaration was pretty cool.*

The point is that there is always a positive side to every unpleasant situation, whether you cause it or not, if you allow yourself to see it. Without knowing that 222 pounds meant more than "a fat body" (because of the information in PJ's book), instead of pouting again and feeling sorry for myself, it helped me find a *positive* even amidst *disappointment*. I could concentrate on the frustration or focus on the positive opportunity. Guess which road I decided to travel? I thank God for Evelyn's book, "A Love Language from the Ageless One Through Numbers."

Linda Mason/ An Author and Publisher

4.

(Spiritual, Relational)

I found myself lost in thought. *'Papa God, the master investment banker, has made deposits in and through us that can not be measured.'* I got it to look at the clock. It was

<u>555</u>

Greater Still
Grace
Greater Still

Speaking of His *grace* being a continuous dividend that goes on and on, we get to enjoy from knowing Him.

P.J. Jefferson/Author

5.

(Spiritual, Physical, Mental, Emotional)

There was a time, at the height of the COVID-19 pandemic, when I felt the need to say to Papa God, although He already knew, but I still felt the need to voice it: regardless of the preventative measures I took, He was the only one I could depend on to keep me. It was clearly evident that this was true because, although I had limited my contact with people, my basic needs still had to be met. I would find people in stores and other places refusing to wear masks, violating my personal space, and failing to sanitize their hands. My family was very concerned because of my health history.

So, during a trip to the grocery store, I observed how people were or were not taking precautions not to catch or possibly spread the disease, which had been responsible for killing thousands worldwide and counting. The store I was shopping in had made it mandatory to wear masks. Even though this was adhered to, upon the customers' entering, I saw people taking them off or wearing them as “neck-kerchiefs.”

As I took in the gravity of the situation, I felt the need to tell the Lord, whom I knew, regardless of how careful I had been; He was the only one I could absolutely, without a doubt, rely on to keep me during this crisis. I’d known of those who had been careful and still ended up with Covid. So, with all my myriad health issues, He was the only absolute protection I could depend on. At the time this took place, He let me see…

<u>555</u>
Greater Still
Grace
Greater Still

Later, to emphasize His confirmation, He brought my attention to

<u>611</u>
I'm covered and
kept by His mercies

But the number between 555 and 611 (on the clock) is 16.

<u>16</u>
LOVE (His love for me and mine)

<u>1</u> Me — <u>6</u> My family

I had a supernatural peace that He had me. 

P.J. Jefferson/Author

6.

(Spiritual, Relational)

03 31 2022

Unlimited God-ordained supernatural unity
Redeemed, recovered, and ultimately
"revealed"

I found myself singing a song to God in my quiet times. The chorus goes

"Light a fire down in my soul that I can't contain
and I can't control
I want more of You, God
I want more of You, God."

He spotlighted these number promises from numbers I encountered during the day

(11) 7	(2) 219 (19)	(10) 102
Guaranteed complete unity victorious connection (7)	Consecrating Faith that secures His & my unity in the future	Testimony of being set apart (2)

0216
Unlimited securing love IS

0727	227 securing (2)
(07)Absolute connection Secured (2) Completely (7)	Revelation that (22) (7) perfects and connects with

How sweet it is when He lets you know He desires the same thing you do, especially regarding your spiritual connection.

P.J. Jefferson/Author

7.

(Spiritual, Physical, Mental, Emotional)

I was on my way to my sister's/publisher's house when, on a long stretch of road, a pain hit my head, and I started feeling a little "off." I could sense a growing panic. I have had a few strokes previously, and even though I've been cleared for years to drive, I'm mindful that if anything suspicious appears, I must do whatever is necessary to keep myself and others safe on the road.

I asked Papa God if I should be concerned. Just as I posed the question, He had me look over to an upcoming roadside marker I was about to pass.

<u>714</u>
Completely SAFE

I smiled, my peace returned, and my symptoms faded away. His number promise brought me peace of mind to resist the fear of the unknown and return to my rest. I absolutely love and adore Papa God's love language to live by.

P.J. Jefferson/Author

8.

(Spiritual, Natural, Mental, Emotional)

03 31 2022

Unlimited God orchestrated miracles for me scheduled for an unbelievable reveal

While working on this book, I was on a phone call when the emergency alarm signal went off in my ear through the earpiece I was wearing to hear my phone calls. It was very unnerving as I have sensitive hearing. Usually, a message would follow to say what kind of emergency we might be dealing with, but there wasn't one this time. A few minutes later, I heard an alarm in my neighborhood. My brother came to my door, saying the news had just been announced that a tornado was on the way and that we needed to relocate to the lower levels of our home. I ended the call and started to head out the door when I saw the time.

<u>0145</u>

Unlimited saving grace

Peace settled as I went downstairs to be with my siblings: two brothers and a sister. The time stamp showed another promise on the clock when I reached downstairs.

<u>0147</u>

Absolutely safe; completely

As we started to take in the updates from the news, we were verbally assaulted with various levels of fear mixed with facts about how safe we were or were not. The news, fearfully, warned that a catastrophe would unfold if we didn't treat it as a specific, immediate life-or-death situation. We could visibly see that the brunt of the crisis on the TV map as it moved away or stayed steady in neighboring communities, as they inferred impending doom. Different stations had different views of the storm's severity, depending on their location. We changed the channel.

On a different local station with an older meteorologist who had been our weatherman for decades, his demeanor was very calm. However, it was still deliberate and thorough, providing accurate information on exactly where the storm was located, its appearance, which landmarks nearby would help you determine its location, and what to expect. It even included a good action plan. He had the peace-filled wisdom that could be felt and trusted. But he had the stamina and delivery speed of a young man.

We settled on that channel and watched the slightest bit of what was thought to be heavy winds and severe downpours move away from our area. The only thing that showed up near our home was a light rain. Other news anchors continued to speak with heightened fearfulness about the impending doom. But before I ever heard the news from someone here on earth, Papa God had given me the truth that

0145 we had	we were 0147
Unlimited	absolutely safe
Saving grace	completely

And it had been
confirmed by the
0333
Omniscient (all-knowing)
God of
God orchestrated miracles

This is why I turned to Him first and depended on what He gave me, regardless of what humans who tout themselves as being "experts"

God is knowledge.

He knows all.

He sees all.

He is the author of time who is more qualified to keep you in "the know."

P.J. Jefferson/Author

(Spiritual, Recreational)

03 03 2022

Unbelievable God orchestrated
Unlimited miracles of redemption
Recovery is yet to be "revealed"

All the numbers in this testimony were times shown on clocks throughout the day.

0556
Unlimited Greater Still
Grace for us

0557
Unlimited Greater Still
Grace to help; perfect, correct, and change things

0558
Unlimited Greater Still
Grace for Nu beginnings

0559
Unlimited Greater Still
Graced future

1
Unifying

310
God orchestrated
Testimony of Greater Grace

2
Set apart by →

225
Securing Redeeming Grace

309	0908
God orchestrated Unlimited future	Unlimited future of Unlimited Nu beginnings

While watching an episode of "The Vampire Diaries," Season 2 (set apart), Episode 14 (to be saved), told the story of someone who learned he had triggered a family curse said to be "irreversible." The writers chose the background music as the song of a well-known Christian artist, Matthew West, "Family Tree." This song talks about how even if you find that generational things try to chain you to a mindset that speaks hopelessness of being "chained" to the accursed situation forever on repeat, that doesn't have to be your "fate" or your "future." You don't have to be chained to live out old baggage from your family's past. It talks about God loving you and waiting to give you "Nu."

New Mind
New Heart
New Understanding
New Beginnings.

You can break the chains of your past and set a brand "Nu" branch of your lineage, with God's help, for others to follow. The time stamps pertaining to this testimony were given to me earlier that evening without explanation of what they meant. I think it's so awesome that Papa would give me the prophetic timestamp messages that matched the song's promise regarding the storyline, which is so relatable to life.

Although I know this to be true, it never ceases to amaze me when Papa God shows that nothing is by chance. He is the author of time.

He is sovereign (almighty).
He is providential (all-seeing, all-knowing).
He is ever-present when needed.

He is the Always-Was and Always-Will-Be God. He knows the root of the matter, and you may have had no part in starting it, but it can be cut if you want. Ask Him, and let Him show you how!!!

P.J. Jefferson/Author

10.

(Spiritual, Relational)

I once called to ask how to write under a pseudonym because of the perceived risk of content from some religious viewpoints, when Papa had me check the time.

<u>0144</u>
Absolutely safe to
create

<u>0147</u>
Absolutely safe
completely to teach,
perfect, correct, protect,
and connect

<u>0153</u>

Unlimitedly restoring
with the unifying grace-filled
divinity of God in us

P.J. Jefferson/Author

11.

(Spiritual and Relational)

While writing about God's desires for loving relationships versus ritualistic religious duty, I saw the following numbers.

0321
Unlimited God orchestrated reunion (securing of unity)

P.J. Jefferson/Author

12.

(Spiritual, Recreational)

How would you feel if you were going through something that was weighing you down, and then decided to play a game on your phone, Xbox, PlayStation, etc.? And then, looking over at your game points, you saw a number like...

17555

Victorious Greater Still Grace Greater Still

His promise of help is waiting. So many encouraging messages are waiting for you, even when you are trying to relax and escape your day-to-day routines during troubling times. Additional encountered while playing this game.

829

Nu beginnings being held in trust for your future

8719

Nu beginnings being perfected for your faith-filled, fruitful future

8

Nu beginnings

7

Perfect

4

Creative

3

Power

3

God

6

You

4336

Creative power of God is at work for you

P.J. Jefferson/Author

13.

(Physical, Mental, Emotional, Financial)

I am Linda, a publishing assistant and author, and I would like to share a couple of short yet powerful testimonies. I am about to have a *'Watchman' procedure, which* requires Medicare approval for billing. Feel free to look it up if you'd like more information. My point for mentioning it is the significance of the "number messages" I experienced throughout the procedure.

This procedure required a pretest CTA before the patient's overnight stay for the Watchman's cardiac procedure. (Computed Tomography Angiography is a type of medical exam that combines a CT scan with an injection of a special dye.) The doctors must submit a request to the Medicare department, which must be approved for payment before either procedure can be performed. The CTA and the Watchman procedure were set a week apart.

I received my approved Medicare financial statement three days before the pretest was scheduled, which indicated that a $5,033 bill was *PAID IN FULL,* with the portion I may owe being "ZERO." The same thing occurred the following week, three days before the

Watchman procedure was scheduled. Medicare approved and paid for a quarter of a million-dollar procedure and an overnight hospital stay in full before the procedure was even done. Have you ever known a doctor or hospital bill to be paid by Medicare before receiving treatment? I have known several individuals who have been denied coverage by Medicare multiple times for specific medical care procedures.

My exact bills looked like this: the first CTA bill was $5,033. Spiritually, the "**50**" part of this number lets me know that the Holy Spirit is with me as my *Day of Jubilee* draws nearer. I *will* be celebrating. The two **3**s confirmed to me that I have a resurrection, retroactive power working on my behalf through an Omnipotent (all-powerful), Omniscient (all-knowing), and Omnipresent (everywhere at the same time) God who is here for whatever I need at this particular time. Can you believe that kind of message of a PAID IN FULL hospital bill can provide me with this much peace?

The second bill for the Watchman procedure was precisely $205,266, for which I owed *nothing*. Spiritually, the "20" part of this number lets me know that

- *I shall "recover, recuperate, and recapture"* my health through this procedure (20)
- *I have grace and favor (5)*

- *I am secured and anchored in Him* (2) or
- *He reminds me again that I am redeemed and shall recover (26)*
- *He reminds me that He's got me as He does with all mankind. (6)*

And just when I thought I'd gotten all I could from God off the *Paid-in-Full* statement, a **"reference #"** was spotted: **1540434,** and I can't forget the **"You Pay $0"** on the statement. The zero reassures me that there are "no boundaries" and limitless possibilities God has in store for me if I allow Him to take me there. He will take me to the immeasurable depths of Him and life. God showed me this by examining this book's zero areas, and He made it personal for "*such a time as this*."

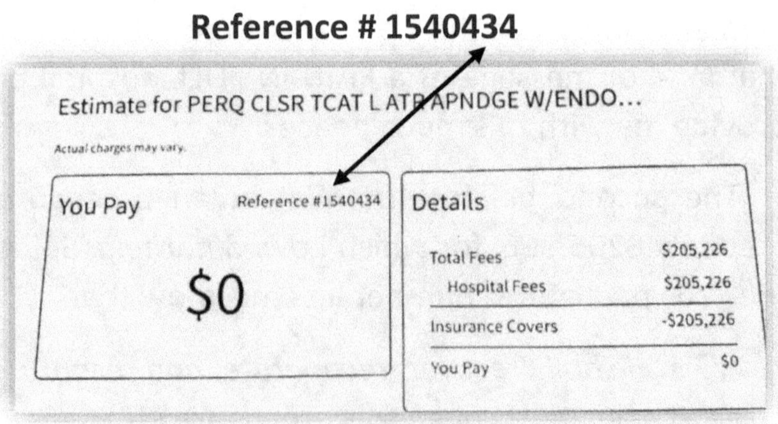
Reference # 1540434

Estimate for PERQ CLSR TCAT L ATR APNDGE W/ENDO...

Actual charges may vary.

You Pay — Reference #1540434

$0

Details

Total Fees	$205,226
Hospital Fees	$205,226
Insurance Covers	-$205,226
You Pay	$0

- **15 =** One of the **rest** acronyms in this area said for me to "**R**elinquish control of **E**verything (including worry) while **S**imply **T**rusting that everything will be alright."
- **40 =** This procedure in the hospital is the end of a specific trial before I'm allowed to enter *"The Promise Land."* My appearance will be transfigured, made over into my *"greater."*
- **4 =** Expect "growth" as I produce exponentially. I was created to expand my boundaries.
- **30 + 4 =** (**30**) I am to rise. I am empowered unlimitedly to increase and prosper others. It's never just about ME. (**4**) A different point than the #4 above it. I need to Invest--- give of myself to

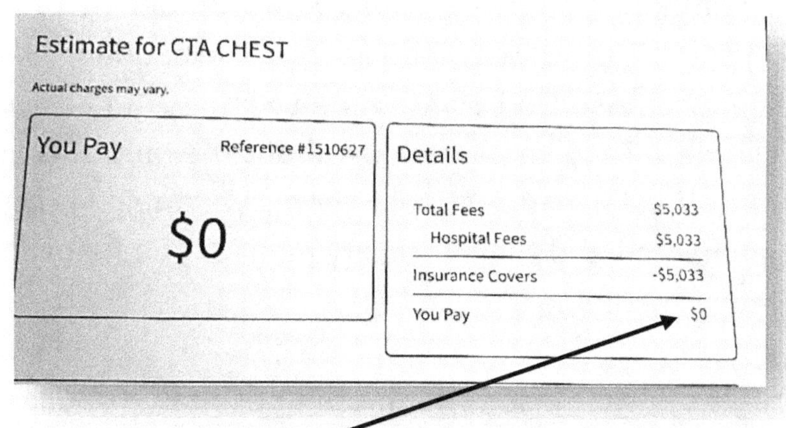

ensure the success of someone or something.

CTA Chest Bill Paid in Full

Wow! Can you believe this fresh revelation, revealed by interpreting the numbers from this book? This stuff is soooooo powerful and undoubtedly full of love!!

{"I believe all of what has been revealed through the number messages from 'A Love Language from the Ageless One' book has already been released into my life."}

I communicated with two other individuals visiting me in the hospital about where I got the confidence that all would be well with me through the heart procedure. When I returned home, I knew I needed to look up my hospital room number (407) in the number's love language book to see what else God wanted me to know. However, my visitors immediately told me to check out two additional numbers: the room number in reverse (704) and the time I was set free from the bedpan, "3:30," to see what else God wanted me to know. Ain't my God awesome!? They knew nothing about the numbers book beyond what I had just told them, yet their faith was supercharged and their curiosity piqued. The following is what was revealed.

4/19/22 **407** (room number in hospital): (**4**) *Change-* the ability to make or become different (**40**) *Transform-* to change in structure, appearance, or character; to makeover (**7**) *Determined-* Firmly resolved to fix the form

or character beforehand and settle it. **704** (hospital room number in reverse): (**7**) *Full*- Things brought full circle; complete (**0**) *Unbelievable*- (except by faith) Things that can take place that you've never heard or seen before, making it hard for you to believe except by trusting what God says or what He shows you is coming.
(**4**) *Increase*- exponential addition

3:30 pm (the time in the hospital when I was allowed to sit up and walk to the bathroom instead of using a bedpan): (**3**) *Resurrection Power*- The ability to bring dead things back to life regardless of how long they've been dead. (**3**) *Reality*- Nothing false, fabricated, faked, or omitted. The full truth. (**3 and 0**) *Raised from obscurity.* (**0**) *Unlimited*- Without limits or restrictions.

It is a sense of reassurance for me to know all of that before and after having a risky cardiac procedure done. Thank God for the comforting *"A Love Language* from the Ageless One Through Numbers" book revelation.

Linda Mason/ An Author and Publisher

14.

(Spiritual, Relational)

I started taking communion some time ago with this in mind. I'd known the traditional way I was taught was to get quiet, and before actually taking the bread, cracker, and wine or juice, you should ensure you are not holding any known sin of unforgiveness or anything of a *not-so-good-natured* before you take communion. This is considered a highly sacred and holy act. Traditionally, there was a particular wording you were told to use (different in different religions) to ensure that your taking communion was honored by God. I had been told about, shown, and participated in this since I was a child. But over the years, as my personal relationship with God grew, He allowed me to see what a ritualistic traditional (set in stone as a duty) looked like versus having a loving, fluid (free-flowing), spontaneous, and never-stale relationship with Him could be. That set the tone for all I'd been taught to do traditionally, because now I could trust coming outside "the box" and going on an adventure with Him, telling me what honors Him.

With this in mind, one day in 2020, I told my Papa Daddy God, "*You are so vast, unlimitedly infinite in who You are and what You've done*." I asked Holy Spirit to remind me of something different every day for a year to prove what I already knew was true. I would treat communion as a celebration of what had been done for me and others, to have what we needed — especially this *love* relationship with Him. And that's precisely what He did. It's been so exciting, never knowing what the focus of my appreciation will be, that I celebrate it, and it continues to be an awe-inspiring, intimate time between Him and me. He has used the love language with the numbers book many times to talk about the communion celebration that came to my heart, which was more than acceptable to Him.

But I felt like on this day, 04/29/2022, what He conveyed to me spoke of His heart for me, and my heart for Him had to be shared. God speaks to me in numerous ways, through the arts, music, movies, and nature. With music, He lets me hear songs played in my heart from all genres: Christian, gospel, soul, jazz, hip-hop, rap, and country. You name it; He uses it because He knows I am open to hearing how He's in it.

On that particular day, I heard a verse of a song by Anita Baker ringing in my heart that simply states, "You bring me joy." I got so excited because I immediately thought how appropriate this was to express my feelings for my Papa Daddy God. As I started writing, I heard Him say that this was a two-way relationship between Him and me and that He felt the same way about me. He then let me see a timestamp confirmation.

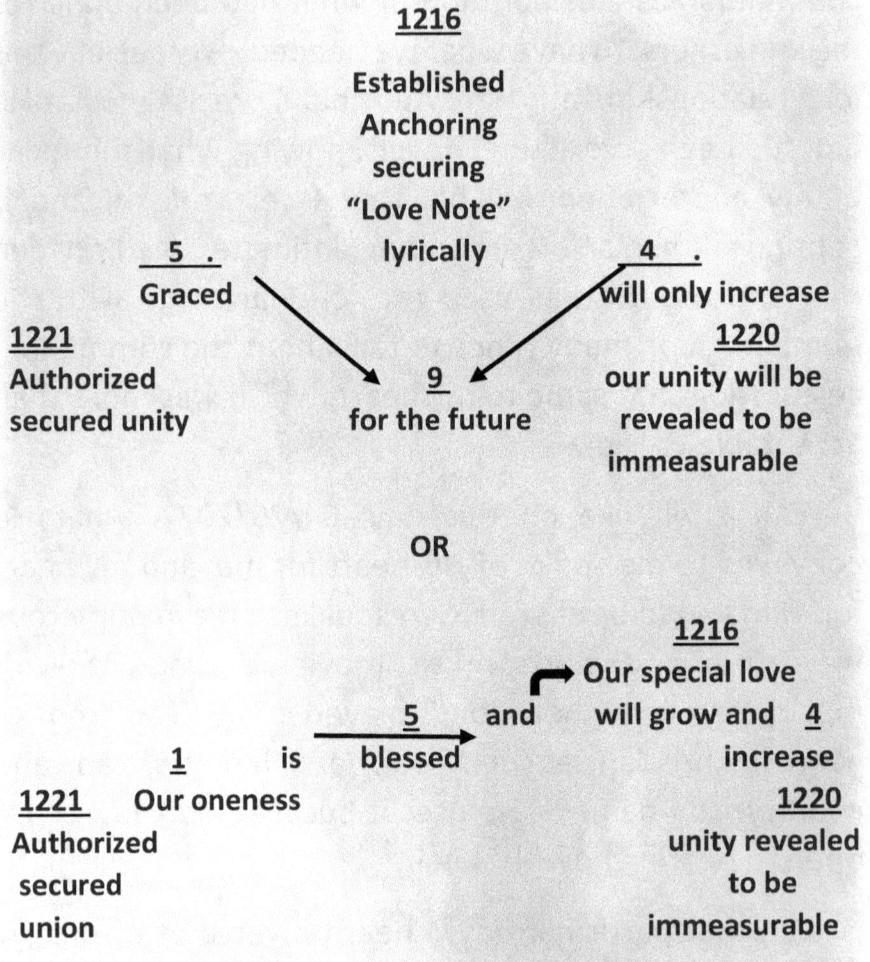

I pray that you don't allow these picture messages to intimidate you. I've been talking with God in this way for years. What started as simple words and phrases has transformed into this. The messages began one number at a time. Those individual number messages added up to life-altering, life-saving, hope-filled, peace-filled promises that took me from death to life.

P.J. Jefferson/ Author

15.

(Physical, Mental, Emotional, Financial)

While trusting God during a season of sickness and being out of work before I was receiving any income, He would give me number messages like:

0711
Absolutely completely being kept and covered

0714
Unlimited and completely being healed

0209
Absolutely secured for a redeemed, recovered, unbelievably, fruit-filled future

0139
Unlimitedly I'm being delivered into a fruitful future

1155
I'm being covered and kept with **Restorative Gr8er Still Grace**

P.J. Jefferson/ Author

16.

(Spiritual, Emotional)

My daughter was joking with me about figuring something out when I got it to look at the clock's time, which was

Authorized 1222
Scheduled reveal

He said I didn't have to try to figure it out. The reveal was on a timer (schedule), and all I had to do was wait.

P.J. Jefferson/ Author

17.

(Mental, Emotional)

At the beginning of learning about the love language through numbers, I was very excited because it was presented in a lovingly and positive manner. I came to understand this as different family and friends went through things like illnesses and losses, divorce, or complicated finances. What Papa God allowed me to understand was how knowing the truth could bring great "peace." Two such incidents occurred when two of my aunts were sick at the same time. One was hospitalized, and it appeared she might not make it. God gave me these different numbers at different times: 13, 14, 20, 25, 40 — deliverance, healing, recovery, recovering grace — and this 40 was "building up" for a return home. My aunt did return home.

Not many months later, she returned to the hospital, and He gave me some of those exact numbers, but this time I heard 13, 40, 18: deliverance into transition, the end of trials and testings, and the end of bondage into a glorious Nu beginning. He let me know He had set the time for her transition to pass on with Him.

1240

Her Time to Transition

God was letting me know that she would pass this time and that all of her struggles would be over. I found comfort in knowing that she would be home with Him.

When the second aunt entered a rehab facility, Papa God gave me the number 40, and I heard from Him that this was her time to transition. He was preparing me for her passing. She, too, was about to experience an end to her ongoing struggles. I appreciated that Papa God would trust me with the "truth" and then allow the truth to bring me comfort and peace.

I was released from the shoulda, woulda, coulda; a simple reveal that He was in this, and it was between them and Him.

I thank Him
for this awesome
way of proving
His love and
care for us.

P.J. Jefferson/ Author

18.

(Mental, Emotional, Financial)

A younger sister/friend was going through a time of unemployment due to illness. My friend, who is like a little sister, was on a fast track in corporate America when the episodes started. Her parents insisted that she move back home with them. A very humbling pill to swallow because of her fierce sense of independence.

She then began the journey of trusting God despite what her situation would say about her future being debt-laden and without a way to return.

She was clinging to Papa's promises and finding peace when she received a student loan bill in the mail. She called me, and when she told me the bill's balance was **$77,777.77**, I smiled and giggled.

WHAT ARE THE ODDS? I saw this,

Everything would be perfectly alright!!!

The 7s were an intentional prophetic promise regarding provision for her future.

7 **7** **7** **7**

Perfecting, Correcting, Completely, Totally,

Predestined, Trustworthy, and Guaranteed

also

God gave me these scriptural promises to go with the prophetic number promises, because she is someone who knows the Bible.

<u>7777777</u>

Psalms 138:8A The Lord will perfect that which concerns me.

Deliverance into

God orchestrated

"Nu" everything

Philippians 4:19 But my God will supply all your
Creative/building needs according to His riches in glory
of faith by Christ Jesus.

Deuteronomy 8:18A But thou shall remember the
Nu creation of Lord thy God, for it is He who
Glorious Nu gives us the power to get wealth.
beginnings

Proverbs 10:22 The blessing of the Lord makes
Glorious reveal (truly) rich, and He adds no sorrow
with it. (neither does **toiling**
increase it.)

To
Overwork and worry yourself,
In hopes that it will
Let you
Increase and really
Never having to depend on
God to make a difference by keeping His promise

Matt. 6:26 Look at the birds of the air.
Your security They neither sow nor reap
for you nor gather into barns, and yet
your heavenly Father takes
care of them.

Psalms 23:1
Secured by God, unique to the need

The Lord is my shepherd.
I lack nothing.

Jeremiah 29:11
Secured future guaranteed

For I know the thoughts and plans that I have for you, says the Lord. Thoughts and plans for your welfare, provision, and peace, not for evil, to give you hope in your final outcome.

P.J. Jefferson/Author

19.

(Spiritual, Mental, Emotional, Relational)

Talking with my daughter about the fear factors concerning everything happening in the world today, I started sharing with her where I am in my life with these concerns. I let her know I was grateful to have been delivered from fear about whether or not I had done enough to change what was happening in the world.

It's been noted that religious leaders have sometimes blamed people for not praying enough, fasting enough, or giving enough time and money to different religious-based organizations and programs as the reason we're in such a mess. And even though I had participated in all of the above, I was left feeling inadequate, as though I was an unfaithful failure.

Since those earlier years, God has freed me from the false responsibilities that others and I held myself accountable for. He made it clear what He wanted from me: to come into agreement with Him whenever given the opportunity, to be faithful with His help, to do what I can when I can, and to stay in peace, knowing that He has the rest, regardless of what it looks like. I have great faith in God's faithfulness.

As I ended the call, God drew my attention, as He often does, to how long we had been talking. It had been 19 minutes and 00 seconds.

1900.

Faith, unlimited for absolutely everything

As He often does with His number messages to me, it made me smile, as He said I had faith unlimited for everything, which was what the conversation had been about. Even though this happens often, it never ceases to amaze me.

P.J. Jefferson/ Author

20.

(Spiritual, Physical, Mental, Emotional)

Current Crisis--- "COVID-19"

Crisis of being at a crossroads re:
Our
Views on
Indivisibility or
Divisiveness when it came to the worldwide family during this life-or-death, troubling time

19- Re: Faith and trust, and in whom would we place our "trust."

It was and is all about faith when the going gets fearfully tough. During this time, we were challenged about whom and what we would trust to get us to the other side of this worldwide pandemic. The fear and disrespect fostered a divisive spirit in how this situation was handled. It raised the question: to whom are you giving the power of your trust?

Truth be told, God is the only one trustworthy enough to place our faith in "*every time*."

P.J. Jefferson/ Author

21.

(Spiritual)

<u>05242022</u>

Unlimited grace for a relationship with the "redeemer" revealed

I was in thought when it came to me to write about how Papa God was the story of our lives. Immediately, my human mind started challenging the statement, since I knew we all have different belief systems. There are so many different ideas of what faith is that I knew I needed proof of my information that would be relatable, regardless of who reads this, and this is what came:

You (God) are the "**story**" of our lives
So, could you please help us tell it?

Strength and solace
Through trials and sorrows, as well as
Our overcoming victorious
Rest that we come to know and understand that
You were in it all!!!

Everybody can relate to having found strength that you didn't know you had when challenged with situations, trials, tribulations, and sorrowful things that threaten to be the end of you. But God, whether acknowledged or not, gave you what you needed, *Grace, Great Grace, Greater Still Grace,* or *Greater Still Grace-Greater Still* that enabled you to overcome and still be here. There's a gospel song that says, "Sometimes I Sit and Wonder How I Got Over," but there is no need to wonder, for it was God.

The number messages came during the time I was writing. The recorded times are spread out because I had been busy doing other things, and then He would let me know He wasn't finished with what I'd written.

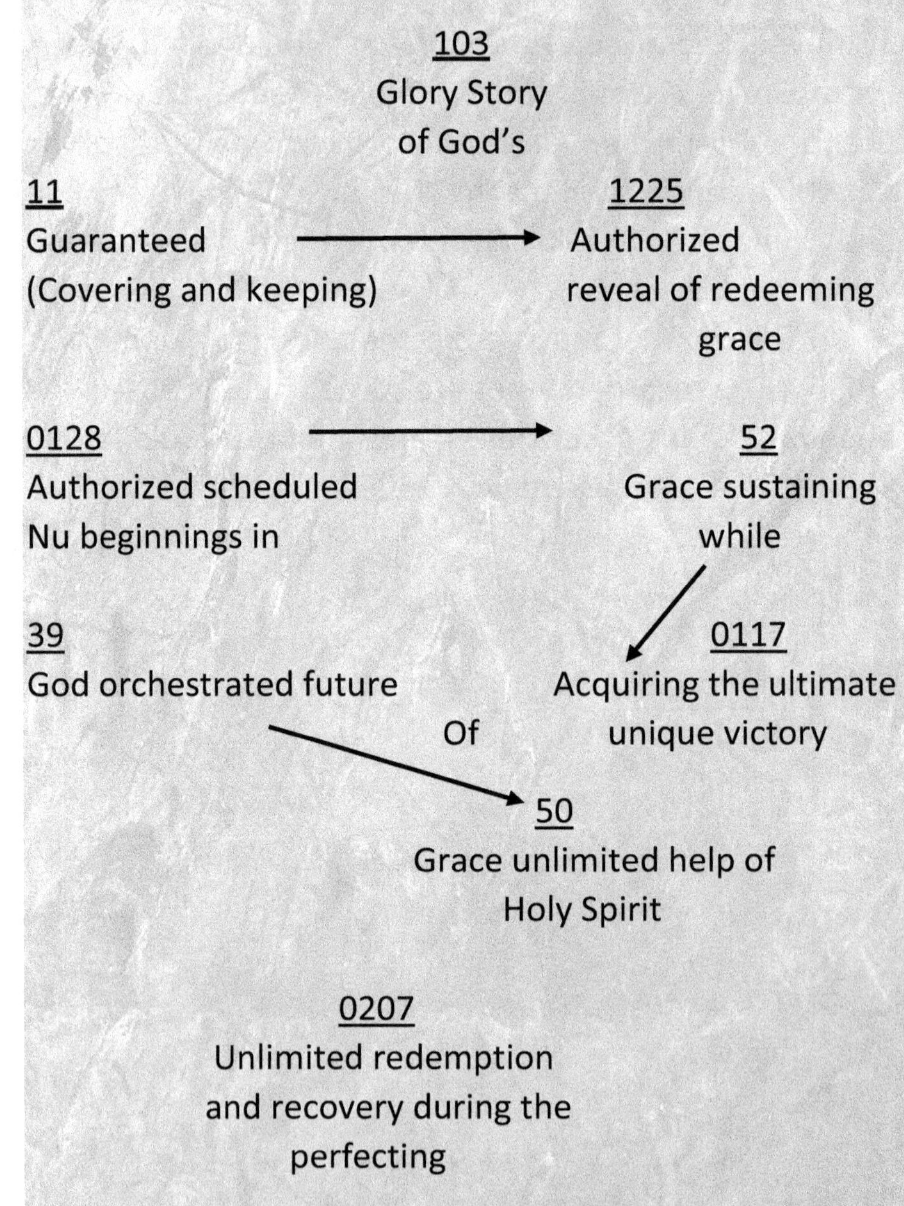
103
Glory Story
of God's
11
Guaranteed
(Covering and keeping)
1225
Authorized
reveal of redeeming
grace
0128
Authorized scheduled
Nu beginnings in
52
Grace sustaining
while
39
God orchestrated future
0117
Acquiring the ultimate
unique victory
Of
50
Grace unlimited help of
Holy Spirit
0207
Unlimited redemption
and recovery during the
perfecting
P.J. Jefferson/ Author

22.

(Spiritual, Mental, Emotional)

A sister/friend and I were discussing her challenges with her three kids on the phone. The challenges were of a nature that a *"one fits all"* answer was not going to cut it. While on the call, she had to stop and give instructions, which seemed to fall on deaf ears. I encouraged her to go ahead and call me back. As the call ended, I saw we had been on the call

2554 25 minutes and 54 seconds.

God said through these numbers that she had "Securing Greater Still Grace" to work with while doing what was needed to bring about change. All those numbers can be found in this number message.

2 = Securing

55 = Greater Still Grace to

4 = Work with until change comes

P.J. Jefferson/ Author

23.

(Mental, Emotional, Opportunal)

I was talking by phone with someone looking to relocate and was not finding anything suitable when I looked down at the phone to see how long we had been on the call. It had been 4055 (40 minutes and 55 seconds), "*Transitional Greater Still Grace*" was the promise. The number 40 can represent "*transition,*" and the number 55 deals with *Greater Still Grace* and speaks for itself. *Grace Greater Still* is for whatever is needed. This number message spoke of the promise that the person would not only find a place to relocate, but that everything necessary to make the transition would be provided by "*Greater Still Grace*."

P.J. Jefferson/ Author

24.

(Spiritual, Mental, Emotional, Relational)

05252022

I was talking to someone with a heavy heart over the report of another school shooting. This time, it was a mass shooting at an elementary school. The worldwide outpouring of pain-filled condolences filled the airways. While we were talking, I checked how long we had been talking. I found that we had been talking for 11 minutes and 27 seconds.

1127

Unifying mercy is securing and connecting us all.

1 – Unifying

11 – Mercy

2 - Securing

7 – Connecting us all

P.J. Jefferson/ Author

25.

(Spiritual, Mental, Emotional, Relational)

On Friday, July 8, 2022, I noticed 05:05 on my cell phone. In short, I immediately knew the Lord had a message for me. I know that 0 means awesome, unlimitedness of God toward me, and all life could hold for me. 5 means grace, favor, and blessing. I knew my day would be filled with God's tangible presence, and I could expect unusual goodness. Everywhere I went, I was blessed with the favor of God. I went to the pharmacy in Amelia and Food Lion for flowers, and when I visited my husband's gravesite, God's tangible presence showed up. I also visited a sister-in-Christ and shared some of the flowers there. The power of God flooded the area, and I spent time there praising the Lord. 05:05 was what I needed to see.

Later, while visiting Petersburg, I saw my brother at the service station. I needed to get my hair done and mentioned it to him. He told me to follow him to the African Braiding Salon. I got scheduled immediately and received a huge discount on the cost due to my brother's business relationship with the owner. Isn't God good? Other significant events took place that day, and I had God's favor. I am so grateful that the Lord loves me and wants to get my attention so I can know His plans for me and my day. These experiences taught me to anticipate His visitation and be ready to respond to Him correctly. I love the Lord so much.

Pattie Hertz

26.

(Spiritual, Opportunal)

One of my own experiences—can't wait to share how God revealed Himself through numbers to me, Pat. There have been many, but this one time still burns in me. God knew I wanted to play the lottery, so I started reading about it and asking lottery wizards (mom, her friend, and aunt) how to do it. I had traveled to another city. While at the gas station, the gas tank number was illuminated. When a car passed, that same number on the license plate illuminated almost as big as the back of the vehicle. I ran into the store, but the cashier was greener than me and didn't know how to do it. I called my aunt in

Petersburg, who told me I needed to play it for three days straight and how to combinate it.

After spending an hour out of town in a strange area working on this lottery number and filling out the card, I finally got to the cashier. I handed her the lottery card and debit card, and she said, "I am sorry, but you must have cash." All the air went out of me, and I got in my car and did the hour-long drive back home. Well, the number did come out.

Today, you can pay with a debit card. OK, this may not be the best experience to share (very selfish), and some may doubt that God was engineering it, but I genuinely believe it was Him, demonstrating that He could give me a winning number. I do not think it was from any other source but God. Following through was my part.

I'll be ready the next time that ever happens to me. It also helped me to trust Him more in other situations in my life. It solidified my understanding that He is not limited to the few ways we have given Him permission to communicate with us.

Pattie Hertz

27.

(Spiritual, Relational, Recreational, Opportunal)

After hearing the tremendous testimony from Tim Tebow, how God used his wanting to bless and encourage people and honor God by wearing scripture in his eye black under his eyes, he started wearing Philippians 4:13. But on Jan. 8th, 2009, he changed it to John 3:16. Exactly 3 years to the day, Jan. 8th, 2012, his team won against the Pittsburg Steelers in the 1st round playoffs.

Before the press interviewed him, his PR person tracked him down to inform him of what he had done monumentally. Regarding the connection to John 3:16, his PR told him during the game---

He threw for 316 yards
His yards per rush were 3.16
His yards for completion were 31.6
The time of possession was 31.06
The ratings for the night were 31.6
90 million people had Googled John 3:16

I got excited about the miraculous number lineup and planned to write about it, but I needed to get something to eat first. I went downstairs to get something to eat and ended up conversing with a family member who was very frustrated regarding being misunderstood. After we talked, I came back upstairs to go ahead and write up Tim Tebow's testimony. I noticed the time when I left was **0217**. I mention this because I started writing when I returned upstairs, but I heard God say, *"Look at the clock."* It was **03:16**.

Even though I'm used to God setting these kinds of things up, it never gets old for blowing my mind. God reminded me that He had told me that the scripture John **3:16** reads, *"For God so loved the world, He gave His only begotten son, that whoever believes in Him shall not perish, but have everlasting life."*

Also meant, "For God so loved the world, He gave us each other." He was reminding me that I had left at **0217**, and now it was **0316**.

0217	**0316**
Ultimate Securing	**Ultimately with God**
Of Unifying Connection	**and with each other**
0 = Ultimately	**0 = Ultimately with**
2 = Securing	**3 = God and**
1 = Unifying	**1 = Each**
7 = Connection	**6 = Other**

He blows my mind every time.

P.J. Jefferson/ Author

28.

(Spiritual, Relational, Recreational, Opportunal)

I was playing a game on my phone when I got a call regarding how some books my sister was working on needed reformatting. Out of nowhere, God connected my sister to what we needed. She could help and went above and beyond what we even knew was needed. We discussed how, through incidents like this, God was assuring us how much He was in this with us through these supernatural provisions. I got it to look at the game on the screen, and at that time, it showed that I had 117554 currency to purchase different kinds of help to win the game.

When I saw it, I heard that this was Papa God's promise of provision to get done all He had put in our hearts and minds to do for Him. He can and will speak through any number at any time. We just need to be available to see and hear what He wants to say.

<u>117554</u>

**Guarantee of Unifying Victorious
Connections with Gr8er Still Grace
to create with**

P.J. Jefferson/ Author

29.

(Spiritual, Relational)

I caught an interview with actor Matthew McConaughey about how his son came to be named "Levi." He said he and his wife discussed it possibly being Matthew Jr., but Levi, another name for Matthew according to the Bible, was among six boy names they were considering. McConaughey said his favorite scripture in the Bible was Matthew **6:22**.

An hour after baby boy McConaughey was born, the doctor handed them a card to fill out. It read.

"Blank was born at ***6:22*** *p.m."*

So they said, "It's Levi."

622

His Name Revealed

P.J. Jefferson/ Author

30.

(Spiritual, Relational, Recreational)

I was conversing with someone about the many challenges facing our nation as a whole and each of us individually, with greater threats emerging every day. But I started talking about how God promised He would keep us who depend on Him, regardless of what we might face from decisions made by those in authority that were not in everyone's best interest. As I started to repeat a particular word, 'promise', I got it to look at the time. It was 01:41.

0141

Absolutely, I Got You

0 = Absolutely
1 = I
14 = Got (Protection)
1 = You

I share this updated promise Papa God made with the *time,* right as we were talking. I'm always in awe when He does this.

P.J. Jefferson/ Author

For Those Who Need to Know

For those who've been looking for the mention of "Jesus" in this book, He is a part of every page. He who is God, part of the God Head, Father, Son, and Holy Spirit, yearns for everyone to know. He is our Savior, Big Brother, who came to model how the Father loves everyone, which religion has failed to do. He, who is God, made flesh and walked among us. He was the payment for all humans. He established, through His sacrificial life of meeting humankind's needs without demanding payment, that showed God's love was available for us all; a life lived to let the masses know they could be reconnected to the origin of who they were for the asking. Jesus paid the ultimate price for this revelation to be known.

But I wrote this emphasizing who was first mentioned in the account of the world's creation. He, the Holy Spirit of God, brought forth the word of God into manifested existence. The first two chapters of Genesis speak of Holy Spirit, who He is, and what He did. He has always been here but barely acknowledged until the New Testament, where Jesus set the time for a formal introduction.

He never left and has forever been doing what He's always done; He brought forth the heart of God into manifested existence and helped us, as creators, do the same. Later, those seeking to be empowered by an encounter with the Holy Spirit waited together in one place for Him to show up and make His presence known.

There is a biblical principle called "1st mentioned." This refers to a person or thing first mentioned in the Bible, Genesis 1:2, at the beginning. The Holy Spirit took God's spoken word and brought creation into being.

He was the One to bring the hidden things from God's heart to the light to be seen by all. The very first "Let There Be" was the manifestation of light itself. He is the One who helps bring forth every "Let There Be" that God has agreed to back. Especially those things that God gave us to speak forth from His will.

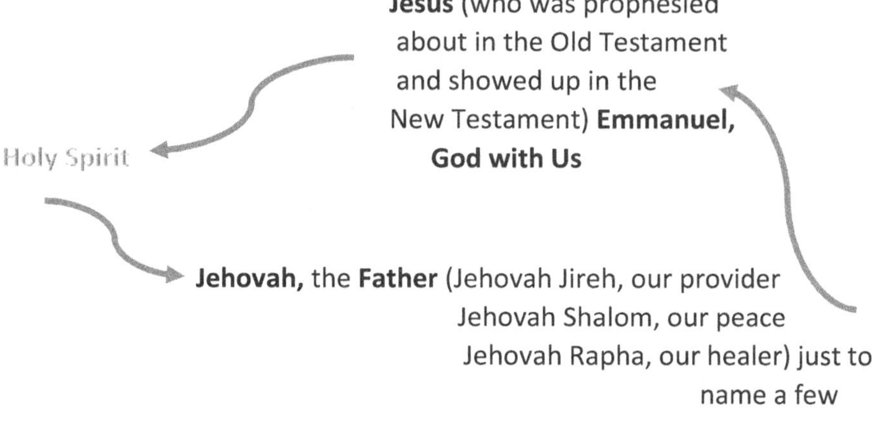

Full Circle Experience with the Godhead:

Father, Son, Holy Spirit

It's time for all to be reintroduced to the Holy Spirit, who is vital to life's essentials.

Acts 2:1-2

Set apart to be unified and consecrated

This is a time for the whole world to know about the Holy Spirit so they can decide once and for all, after knowing who He is and how He is the very essence of life, if they want His help. He's our link between heaven and earth.

St. John 16: 7-9

Love for togetherness

Unity of all mankind

Perfected for connectivity for living

Jesus agreed that it was time for the Holy Spirit to be revealed. In John 4:24, Jesus said there would come a time when people would acknowledge that God is Spirit, and that there would be those who would worship (extravagant respect, reverence, honor) Him in **Spirit** and in Truth.

Space that
Pertains to the
Intimate
Recesses of your
Innermost being
That's untouchable except by the Spirit

Jesus spoke of Him and His importance. The Holy Spirit is the revealer and convincer of Jesus's realness. I trust He will do this and everything else Jesus said He would. I received God's permission to proceed in this manner.

Jesus has been misrepresented so often, even perverted at times, up until now, that this goes without saying: He depends on the Spirit of Truth and those who love Him to convey, by His Spirit, who He really is.

<u>0308</u>

Awesome God
Unveiling
Unlimited "Nu"

Psalms 24:1 (AMP)

Securing creation through relationship for unity

"The earth is the Lord's and the fullness of it, the world and they who dwell in it."

We all belong to Him by His acknowledgment. Now, it's about whether you agree with this revelation of being His that you would be ready and willing to yield to love and be loved. Do you want to, with knowing intention, become one of Papa God's children? He sees you that way now, but He awaits your free will decision, hoping you will develop a desire to know Him and acknowledge you need Him.

God's love is balanced.

- Pure with no hidden motives
- Compassionate, meaning understanding
- Unconditional, meaning unearned, no need to attempt to work for it
- Accountable, to be held responsible
- Immeasurable, covering all He created
- Righteous in His disciplines
- God's love is for everyone, but the greatest of these is God's love for everyone.

Accountability is

Heaven's Growth Hormone for us here on earth.

Heaven's
Growth
Hormone

Just know that God will never ask anything of us
He has not
already done Himself.

He is the epitome of accountability. He has made a pact with Himself to love us for eternity. He holds Himself accountable to His love for us. His love is not conditional on our loving Him back. He reminds Himself of how our fallen state has weakened and pities us. So, He offers us the opportunity to recognize our need for Him. Then He waits for our response to invite Him into our intimate space (our hearts) to begin a conscious, aware relationship, getting to know what His love and care look like through the cleared-up perception of Him. He's been there all along. It's just that the eyes of our hearts are blinded to the truth.

In 1 John 4, it says He gave us the ability to love because He loved us first. In 1 John 4:8, He states that the one who does not love has not become acquainted with God [does not and never did know Him], for God is love.

He is the originator of love, the enduring attribute of His nature.

Isaiah 49:16 (AMP)
Creative Fruit-filled
Love to unite all mankind

"Behold, I have indelibly imprinted (tattooed a picture of) you on the palm of each of my hands."

How encouraging is it to know that the Almighty Creator of all submits Himself to accountability with His love and in remembrance that we are His creations? God does not discard us for not being perfect. He knows that only the perfecting love of God, when yielded to, can perfect us. We can't do that on our own. So, it is left to us to submit ourselves to love, perfecting our ability to love appropriately: God, ourselves, and each other. So, why not submit to love?

MATCHING FRIEND REQUEST

Never had a relationship with God?

From God to You

From the heart of God
Requesting you consider His
Invitation to
Experience a relationship
Not based on what you
Do or don't do, but on

Receiving and responding to His
Eagerness to answer
Questions leading to your
Understanding how
Easy it can be to
Settle and snuggle into a love relationship you can
Trust

From You to Him

First, I need to know You're
Real, so,
I'm asking You to let me
Experience You in a way that there is
No mistaking it's You
Demonstrating in some

Real way that is
Easy for me to know without
Questioning that it was You letting me
Understand how
Easy and
Simple You made it for me to
Trust You.

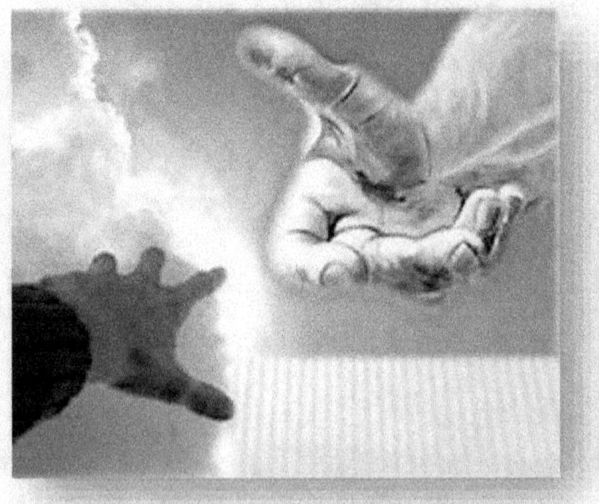

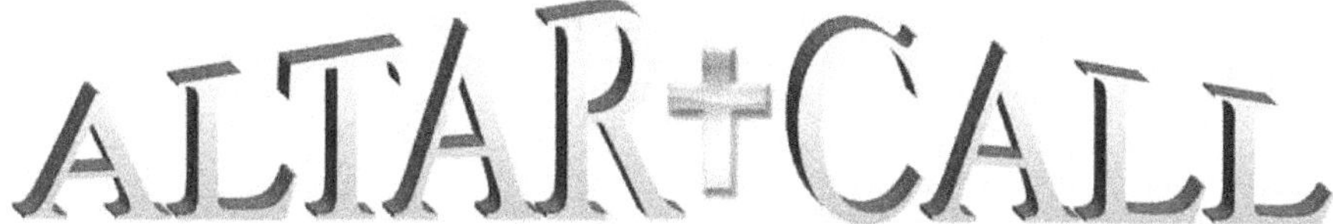

For Those Who are More Familiar with this Term

A time to
Lay everything down
That's hurting you
And practice
Relying on God, who loves you more than you could ever fully know. It's unlimited, and it's unconditional. Don't attempt to work for it. It's wasted time. It hurts God's heart that you would think and feel you need to do that from lies you've been told.
You only need to...

Come into
An agreement to
Let Him
Love you.

I Will STAND on My WATCH and SEE What the Lord Will SAY to Me

Stay still.
Take time to
Acknowledge the
Need to
Daringly,

Wherever I Am,
Ask for
Truth so I
Can
Hear the

Soundness of our
Eternal
Everlasting Father,

So, I can
Agree and give my
Yes, to His will for my life.

Let's Prove to The Whole World God will Speak to Anyone Who Would Listen

1. By sharing additional words or phrases that God revealed to you and that are not in this book, and that spoke to you in your situation, language, culture, and personal understanding of Him, is proof that He can and will speak to anyone.

2. Your stories worldwide will prove that God is everywhere and ready to reveal His caring to anyone who wants it, regardless of race, religion, gender, or age.

3. Help me spread the awesome truth that God is not just interested in communicating with a chosen few but desires loving, vibrant relationships with everyone. Share your encounters and help me prove it.

Afterword

You are already more than you could ever know; even those with a good sense of themselves have so much more on the inside--- "more" than they could ever imagine. You are more than

Thoughts
Words
Actions
Opinions
Environments
The sum of your rights
The sum of your wrongs.
You are greater than any earthly wealth.
You are greater than any perceived achievements.
You are definitely greater than any perceived failures, and perceived losses.
You are more than any short-sightedness regarding your worth that may be on a
forever looping *soundbite* about who you are or are not, or
what you can or cannot be or do---
just know that God said you are loved and "More Than Enough."

To truly know what time it is, I encourage all to go and listen to a song by Larnelle Harris,

called

"Mighty Spirit."

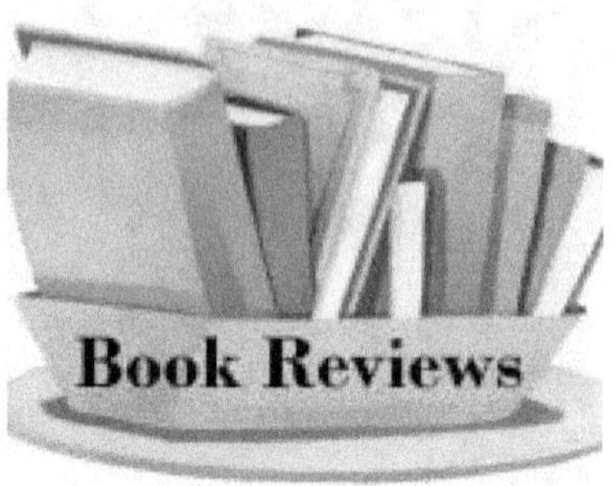

The book is absolutely awesome and done so professionally. My heart fills with joy knowing that this book has been published. I believe it will bless millions and was released at the right time. The personal testimonies and writings about her intimacy with God will cause others to be jealous and desire to develop and deepen their own real-time with the Lord throughout a typical day.

Is it possible to hear from God using numbers? P.J.'s selection of the cover page provides a canvas that sweeps like a brush of revelations concerning numbers intended by God for us to envision. God's love reaches us in every way imaginable as He desires to have us close to Him in the most intimate way possible. Open your heart as you look through the small window and see eternal darkness (before time) when the earth was void. Just as God created the earth, the picture shows the creation of numbers coming from the Ageless One. See the numbers from the light of God as they permeated from the galaxies with a great and mysterious calculation of what the Lord was saying --- and through revelation, we can make it a part of our everyday lives. Yes, allow God to use numbers in your life to be a timestamp on current and future events or creations.

Thank you, Pat, so very much for persevering with the heartfelt leading of the Holy Spirit to see through its first version. It is a transforming book that transcends time, and the timing is perfect. People are hungry for knowledge, as this world's temporal things are less fulfilling to their physical appetites. The desire to know and understand more spiritual things is apparent in the markets of mankind. I wanted so much for this book to be in the hands of the world because I desperately wanted it for myself. The revelation I received through its meaning started another revelation in other facets of my circumstances.

Pattie Hertz
Motivational Speaker and Author of "Daily Living"

ABOUT THE AUTHOR

Evelyn "P. J." Jefferson

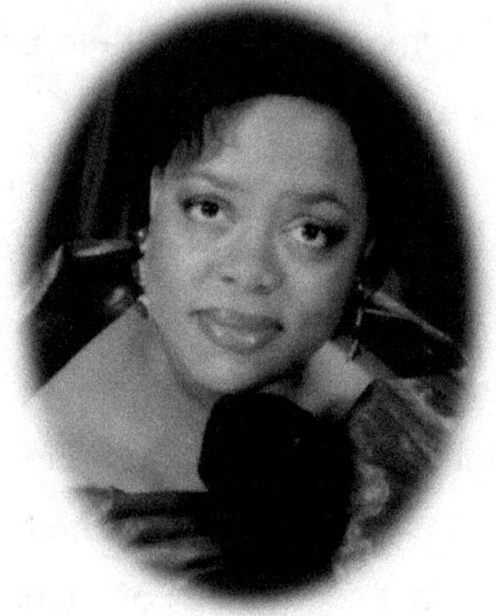

"P. J." has over thirty years of experience in the medical field. She is a retired Licensed Practical Nurse (LPN) and resides in Richmond, VA.

She is the mother of an amazing woman of God, Kalisha Jefferson (a graduate of Regent University), and the grandmother of an astounding young man, Joshua.

Over many years and through inconceivable physical challenges, "P.J." has developed a unique relationship with the Lord, "*her Papa.*" And from that personal relationship and continued communication, several titles for multiple future publications have been birthed, including an "I AM" children's collection. A few other titles are listed below.

- A Fresh Look at the Names of God
- What a Prophetic Word is Meant to be From A-Z
- I Am a Gift from God to You
- Are You Hooked on Political Crack

Just to name a few, and many more.

Your Personal Notes

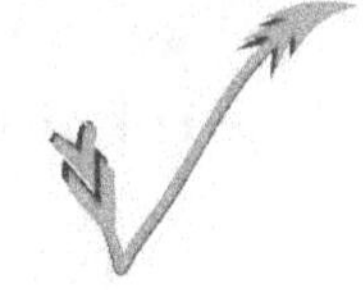

Your Personal Notes

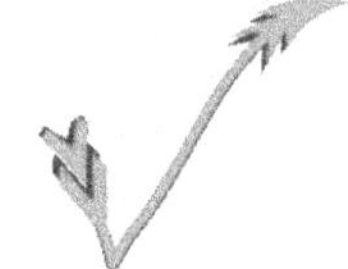

Your Personal Notes

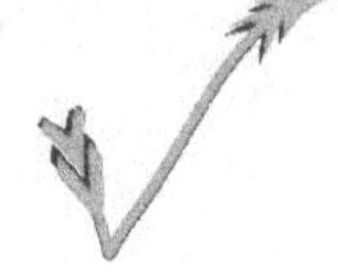

Your Personal Notes

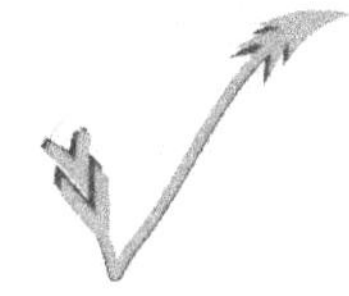

Your Personal Notes

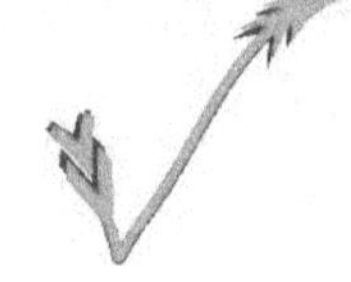

Your Personal Notes

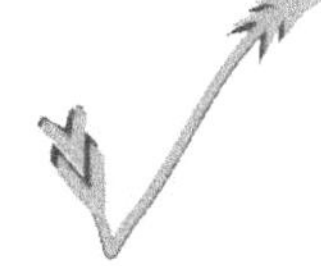

Your Personal Notes

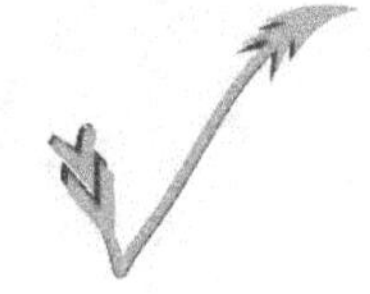

Your Personal Notes

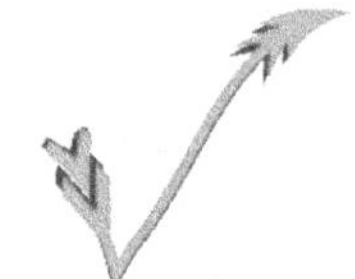

Your Personal Notes

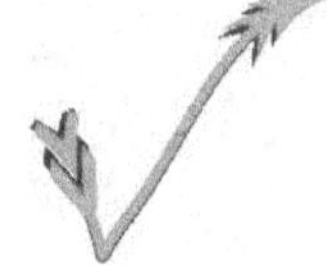

Your Personal Notes

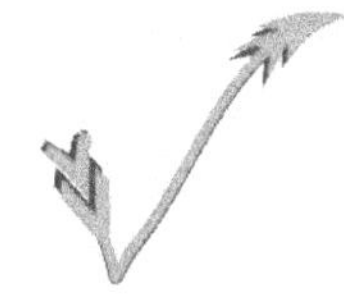

www.ingramcontent.com/pod-product-compliance
Lightning Source LLC
LaVergne TN
LVHW020647110826
845149LV00012B/1935

* 9 7 8 1 9 6 7 2 0 5 5 1 6 *